KEEPER OF LOST PLACES

Matthew Steven Bruen

ROTHCO PRESS • LOS ANGELES, CALIFORNIA

For Jackie, Emmaline, and Phebe

KEEPER OF LOST PLACES

Published by
ROTHCO PRESS
1331 Havenhurst Drive #103
West Hollywood, CA 90046

Cover Design: Rob Cohen

Rothco Press is a division of Over Easy Media Inc.
www.RothcoPress.com
@RothcoPress

Keeper of Lost Places
Paperback ISBN: 978-1-945436-36-9

Table of Contents

Introduction

Let us go then, you and I,
When the evening is spread out against the sky
Like a patient etherized upon a table;
Let us go, through certain half-deserted streets,
The muttering retreats
Of restless nights in one-night cheap hotels
And sawdust restaurants with oyster-shells:
Streets that follow like a tedious argument
Of insidious intent
To lead you to an overwhelming question ...
Oh, do not ask, "What is it?"
Let us go and make our visit.
— T.S. Eliot, "The Love Song of J. Alfred Prufrock"

I.

Lost places are everywhere, you just need to know where to look. And that's what this book seeks to do: it brings you on a literary and photographic journey to ten lost American places. Along the way, you will learn how to identify lost places yourself, so that you might undertake a similar study as the one I present to you in these pages.

My name is Matt. I am a professor, but at heart I am a child with an intense curiosity about the world. I grew up in the Pocono Mountains of Northeastern Pennsylvania. Even then, I was drawn to the abandoned houses and cabins that litter the woods of my home area. Back then I did not know how to talk about the lost places I encountered. Now, however, I am a seasoned researcher with expertise in American history, ecology, and economy.

I think of myself as a keeper of lost places. I find them, I travel to them, I explore them, I photograph them, and then I author essays that tell their stories to my readers. By doing so, I ensure that despite their lost-ness, these places will never be forgotten. I memorialize them through my experiences with them and through the act of writing about them. But this is a two-way street. If no one reads about them, the places remain lost.

That's where you, the reader, comes in. By engaging with the lost places in this book, you too become their keeper. Together, then, we participate in a beautiful memory-building process that keeps the lost alive in our hearts and minds.

I want to thank you for your willingness to become a keeper like me. The places in this book deserve to have their stories told and remembered. They are sites of human experience – of love and death, of progress and backsliding, of the construction of our American nation. Without them, we very well might not be here. So thank you, once again, for coming along on this journey with me.

II.

Before we begin, however, I would like to teach you a few things about places. This will help you better understand the stories to come.

So, to begin: what is place? This seemingly innocuous question has stymied place theorists for decades. In fact, many studies of place fail to successfully move beyond the difficult problems of definition, collapsing in on themselves in a sea of uncertainty and doubt. In particular, studies of regionalism and literary production fall prey to this trap. For others, like Bachelard's obsession with home in his seminal work The Poetics of Space, place becomes wrapped up too narrowly. Others, like Lefebvre, gesture toward place and then abandon it in favor of its cousin, that other devilishly difficult concept called space. Perhaps the most convincing definition of place comes from the cultural geographer Yi-Fu Tuan, who argued in his Space and Place: The Perspective of Experience that place is a special kind of object, invested with symbolism and meaning by human beings (space is that which exists between places in this definition). I don't know about you, but I am still not satisfied with this.

So. To ask the question again: what is place? On one hand, the answer is obvious. Place is "the where." It's where you are, it's where we are, it's where they are. It's where things happen. As the great place philosopher Edward Casey wrote in 1997's The Fate of Place: "To be at all – to exist in any way – is to be somewhere, and to be somewhere is to be in some kind of place." But it's even more than that. Much, much more. First of all, place is a decidedly human construction; if there are no humans, there are no places. Our ability to invest our surroundings with abstract thinking and symbolism is something that separates us from other animal species. For a hummingbird, a flower is just a feeding spot; for a human, a flower is a place of beauty. Places are distinctly human creations. To repeat: if there are no people, there are no places.

As I see it, then, place is how our brains interact with the environments we encounter. Place is our interface with the world. It is the prism through which all of our existences pass. So that's the definition of place that anchors this book: it is our interface with the world.

III.

Not only would we be lost without our places, but our places can very easily be lost themselves. Imagine, for example, your favorite childhood place. Mine was a particular tree bent in the shape of an L that grew in the forest behind my house in the Poconos. I would travel through the woods as a child and always manage to find the L tree. I would climb onto it and sit and read books and watch birds and otherwise enjoy the freedom of being alone in the wilderness. But today, that tree is no longer there. It is gone. It is lost. Such is the way of nature: the planet keeps spinning, you get older, things disappear. I'm sure you have something similar in the vaults of your memory.

In this book, though, I focus predominantly on human settlements of various sizes, including towns, regions, and institutions like resorts and hotels. The size and breadth of these lost places lend themselves to storytelling. Here is a brief description of the lost places featured in the pages to come.

I begin by taking you to my homeland: the mountains of northeast Pennsylvania and northwest New Jersey. Along the banks of the Delaware River a horrible drama played out in the middle of the twentieth century. In order to make room for a massive dam, the federal government of the United States displaced over 15,000 residents of the region once known as the Minisink. But then something unexpected happened...the United States never built the dam in question. Eventually, the contested territory was turned into public land administered under the National Park Service. To this day, the Delaware Water Gap National Recreation Area is home to hundreds of abandoned farmhouses, barns, mills, forts, and other structures. It is as if time stopped in 1965.

In the book's second chapter, I take you on a guided trip to Centralia, Pennsylvania, a former coal town located directly in the heart of the Keystone State's anthracite country. The residents of Centralia accidentally lit a coalseam on fire – an event that led to the wide-scale destruction of their town. To this day, if you look hard enough, you can find smoke rising up from cracks in the ground in the woods around Centralia. It's as if hell opened up right beneath them.

We then move down through the mid-Atlantic to the Susquehanna River town of Lapidum, Maryland. Unlike most of the places featured in this book, Lapidum is completely destroyed. Only a few feet of canal and the stone foundation of a hotel are left. The agent of its destruction was a massive flood of ice that washed down the big river. It took everything with it, including most memories of what Lapidum used to be.

We continue to move south in the book's fourth chapter, which provides a snapshot of life in the Copper Basin. This region straddles the border between Georgia and Tennessee. It was the site of much tragedy and sadness, including an illegal adoption ring that created huge ripples across space and time. Like Centralia, the Copper Basin has also fallen victim to environmental degradation. The regular atmospheric release of sulphuric acid from factories in the Copper Basin has left the region permanently scarred.

In the fifth chapter, I bring you to Haydenville, Ohio, a former factory town located about an hour and a half south of Columbus. The former residents of Haydenville were master brickmakers. Haydenville bricks can be found all over the world, including in Savannah, Georgia and in some European cities. When I take you for a walk along the streets of this town, you will see how the owner of the brick factory used the construction of his workers' lodgings as a gigantic advertisement for his company's business. And when we journey through an abandoned tunnel, you will see and feel the devastation wrought by the globalized, postindustrial economy.

Next, we move to the space that was once known as the North Shore but is now called the Great Smoky Mountains National Park. Here, I will show you how wave after wave of displacement has forever changed life in this slice of the Southern Appalachian Mountains. I will also bring you to one of the largest dams in the Eastern United States. This chapter provides a wonderful "what might have been" with respect to the chapter on the Minisink, in which the giant dam was NOT built. Read with the book's opening essay, this chapter reveals the dark side of America's beloved and cherished public lands.

We then travel back to the northeast, to the place where I grew up. Littering the landscape of the Pocono Mountains are several abandoned resorts. Remnants of an illustrious tourist past, these ghostly campuses are a stark reminder of how changes in the American economy deeply affect everyday life. I bring you inside several of these lost resorts, showing you the visceral and sad state of a once proud and thriving industry.

We return to the Southern Appalachians in the book's next chapter. Here, I take you to visit the site of a long lost civilization of the Mississippian Indians. Not much is known about these enigmatic people, aside from the knowledge that they constructed large and impressive pyramid-like mounds. During our time at this lost place, I put on my archaeologist hat and show you how you can recover lost histories when all you have at your disposal are tiny pieces of material culture left behind by the ancients. I also show you how to think about the former human inhabitations of the pre-Columbian North American continent. The lives of the people who lived here before European colonization were rich, complex, and diverse. And yet, their history remains one of the least explored of all elements of world history. Together, you and I will work to remedy this fact.

The book's penultimate chapter takes us underneath Dulles International, one of the world's busiest airports. To make way for this gigantic piece of American infrastructure, the federal government displaced the town of Willard, Virginia. Almost all of Willard's residents were Black. This is a heartbreaking trip, but very much a necessary one. The experience of Willard shows that what white people in America want, white people in America get – frequently at the expense of minority populations. Yet, I excavate the experiences of the Black citizens of Willard to show you what American life is like when it is left undisturbed and unmolested.

And finally, the book ends with an essay on my ancestral home-town of Waterloo, New Jersey. This is one of the only lost places featured in this book that is being actively restored and maintained. Its story shows how connected human beings become to places and the lengths to which they are willing to go to keep them alive.

IV.

We are almost ready to start out on our adventure. However, there's one more piece of context that I want you to have before we begin.

My travels have taught me that there are three main reasons that American places become lost.

The first is economic decline. This is the main reason that led to the loss of the Copper Basin, Haydenville, and the resorts of the Poconos. It is a secondary factor in all of the other cases. And in this age of MAGA and resentment and Hillbilly Elegy, it seems somewhat trite and banal to blame globalization, yet it is neverthe-less true. Consider the Pocono resorts for a moment. They used to be an easy train ride away from New York City in the early 1900s. When Route 80 was opened through the Water Gap in 1953, city dwellers could then drive to the resorts. However, in today's world, why would NYC's car-less residents vacation in the Poconos when they can board a cheap flight to the Caribbean? I may be one of the only people on the planet that would prefer a Pocono swamp to, say, the sun and sand of Jamaica. So without going down the economic rabbit hole further, it is safe to say that change in the structure of the American economy is perhaps the most powerful factor behind the loss of American places.

The second reason is also straightforward: government malfeasance. This is particularly true in the case of the Minisink. Nothing short of complete and utter stupidity on the part of the federal government is to blame for the loss of that region. It is also true of the North Shore communities displaced to make way for Fontana Dam and the Great Smoky Mountains National Park. At the very least, the families of the displaced were promised a road that would run on the north side of Fontana Lake, so that they could regularly observe the Appalachian tradition of Decoration Day at the cemeteries that contain their dead relatives. Of course, the road was never built, except a stretch called "The Road to Nowhere," located outside of nearby Bryson City. My good friend says that the United States is like a cannibal and that what it eats is itself. Such is the case for the Minisink and the North Shore.

And third: disaster, both man-made and natural. Lapidum, Maryland was mostly abandoned when an ice gorge descended down the Susquehanna River and wiped out all of its structures. Yet, the disaster was a final exclamation point for the loss of that particular place. And of course Centralia, the site of an ongoing underground coalseam fire, was destroyed by its own peoples' ignorance and disrespect of the environment (a disrespect, by the way, that was completely encouraged and supported by the mining companies that dominated those peoples' lives).

To repeat. The three main factors behind the loss of American places are the following: economic decline, government malfeasance, and disaster. We will encounter all of these, over and over again, throughout the subsequent pages.

V.

It's time now. I'm ready and I hope you are as well. So let's head out to our first destination: the rolling green hills of the Valley of the Minisink.

The Lost Region:
The Valley of the Minisink

The past carries with it a temporal index by which it is referred to redemption. There is a secret agreement between past generations and the present one. Our coming was expected. Like every generation that preceded us, we have been endowed with a weak Messianic power, a power to which the past has a claim. That claim cannot be settled cheaply.

— Walter Benjamin, Theses on the Philosophy of History

I.

This is a story about a place, one that was destroyed by a deeply sad amalgam of power, greed, incompetence, and indifference. This is a story about a place that's remains are haunted by ghosts; shades of crumbling structures, of the dead, of peaceable life in the American nation – all these dwell within it.

This is also the story of a place once called region, before condemnation and suicide allowed the forest to creep back into the cropfields and those with no sense of the tragedy of the past rendered it their natural plaything. That is this place, where the western plateau and the eastern mountains are married together by the shallow yet wide river the native peoples called Lenapehanna, a river so basic to their existence they named it after themselves. This is a story of that river and this place, and of how the attempted mastery of the water precipitated a great and still unknown tragedy.

This is the story of what some call the Tocks Island Dam Controversy. But as one of the last keepers of this lost place, as one whose very life has sprung from its soil, I know that there's more to its story than this name suggests. And I wish to tell you of it, so that you might know what happens when a place dies.

II.

When seeking a lost place, it is best to start at a graveyard. There's something about the removal of the dead from the soil that disgusts us, so that even after destruction and ruin rain down, graveyards have a way of remaining untouched until the last. And within, on the stones, are attempts to record the facts of human life and death. Names and dates – places, too. These marks are the last vestiges of real lives, of those who breathed, loved, suffered, and, perhaps, near the end, hated. Collected and contemplated together, these communities of the dead reveal the very fabric of life in a lost place. So let's start this story there, in a graveyard outside of what used to be a town, where the adjacent Flat Brook offers a constant, babbling dirge to those who lie nearby.

These names begin the story: Rosenkrans, Van Campen, Losey, VanHorn, Van Gordon. The Dutch were the first European settlers of what became known as the Minisink, arriving in the seventeenth century from the land of the Hudson. It was to there that they were culturally and economically tied, not to the Quaker city that would later emerge one hundred miles downstream. These were frontiersmen, farmer-folk who moved into the fertile valley between the plateau and the mountain when the wolf and the mountain lion and the Lenape still lived there.

Big, tall chestnut trees filled their woods, with canopies so thick sunbeams rarely reached the forest floor. Along the rivers and ravines, the hemlock loomed just as high, while birch, aspen, hickory and poplar grew in the spaces in between. Below, the multi-colored wildflowers of spring – miterwort, wild orchid, starflower, violet, anemone, and hepatica – chased the sunlight as the chestnut leaves grew, slowly giving way to the nightshades and baneberries of summer. When fall arrived, so too did blazing goldenrod and erratic, haunting witch hazel. These were primeval woods, not yet New Jersey or Pennsylvania: forest, only.

And they were dangerous woods. The Hollanders withstood poison-choked underbrush and the accompanying stings, bites, and scratches of the land they cleared. Wielding giant axes and saws as long as two people, they broke bones and ripped their muscles felling the chestnut and the hemlock, so that they could build houses with lowly sloping Dutch roofs. In the fields that had once been forests, they removed the glacial legacy from the ground, building forlorn rock walls that still divide the land today. And always, always, the wide and shallow river we now call the Delaware, threatened.

This is an ancient river, as old as North America itself. When it first flowed, during those millions of years when no humans lived, it fell to the north. And then, not that long ago, when the human ancestor was first learning the art of speech, it was claimed by a southern river, the two were fused, and together they birthed one of the most marvelous natural wonders in the world: the Delaware Water Gap. All that water, it turns out, was so powerful it cut the Appalachian mountain chain in half. And, as has been the case for millennia, when that water leaves its banks, sheer hell ensues.

The Van Campens and the other families from Holland knew this. The river helped them survive, provided them with fertile floodplain cropfields, with fish and power and transportation, but it was always a danger. So, like the Lenape before them, they were quietly deferential to the shallow yet wide river. Not everyone who came after was. That is a key to this story.

But we must leave these people of the sloped roofs, to whom my great-great-great-great-great grandmother belonged, and remove to the graveyard by the Flat Brook.

Again, let's look to the names on the stones. Placed on nearly half, and on many of the surrounding ravines, towns, and streets, are these: Cole, Bell, Fuller, Tillman, Garris, Layton. These were the English, some of whom were descendants of those who saw God in the flutter of every leaf, who believed that He resided in their very own hearts. Others were branches from peasant-stock, those who had fled the landed gentry of their ancestral homeland. Proscribed from the deer-filled forests and trout-strewn streams of England and forced to work land that was not their own, these peasants migrated, as humans have done since before we were even human, in search of full bellies.

Puritan and peasant descendants alike, the Anglo-Saxons came to the land between the plateau and the mountains seeking a place to farm maize and wheat, where the bounty of the river was theirs to capture and the game of the forest was theirs to shoot. In this place, they lived alongside the Dutch, the Lenape, and even a few Huguenots, intermarrying when this was still unheard of, a bold breaking of tradition that ultimately gave me, and thousands of others, life.

These lovers of tea (for even the North American English loved tea, even the kind made from hemlock needles) built stone homes with river clay as mortar, more to block cold air than to bind rock, and introduced livestock to the region. Soon, they erased the wolf and mountain lion from the forest, defending their life-giving sheep and pigs and cows with bullets. Several decades later, when they had stopped calling themselves Europeans but weren't yet Americans, they took up arms against the human natives, drawing blood and prompting a terrifying conflict that ended, as so many of this story's threads do, in the displacement of peoples.

But before this war, as one century came to an end and another began, the children of Hollanders and Englishmen (and a few brownskin Lenape, we mustn't forget) built the Minisink's first villages. Full of one and a half story cottages with big pane windows that let in the light of the sun, settlements began sprouting up along river bends, near islands, and, closer to the water gap, alongside the creek that bears the maiden name of my great-great-great-great-great grandmother. There, they built churches with even bigger windows, so that the words of their Bibles could be illumined by the sunshine, and they built inns to house those who had begun to travel to their growing region, and, as the old began to perish and the young sought places to remember them, they built graveyards on the edges of their villages, like the one by the Flat Brook.

These multiethnic descendants of the first white settlers raised corn and wheat, while others grew apples to turn into that most American of drinks: hard cider (and, of course, the ensuing applejack). Still others sent thousands of felled trees down the shallow river to new cities hungry for resources, or tanned the hides of dead cattle in stews of hemlock bark and water. All of this – and more. It was a new region, a new place: the Valley of the Minisink.

III.

All that water, so important to life; and yet, so deadly. In 1955 the water left its banks, as it had in 1942 and in 1903 and in 1867 and in the time of the Lenape and in the era of the Amerind and in the millions of years before humans. The result of two back-to-back tropical systems, this latest great flood killed over one hundred people, including thirty children who had come to pray to God in the thick woods, alongside a clear, beautiful creek that turned into anything but. Amid drowned children and a billion dollars of damage, cries rang out: we must do something about all that water!

What happened next is an American tragedy.

I begin by relating an experience told to me by a friend, someone whose life was profoundly shaped by the events that are to be detailed in the lines to come. In the mid-1960s, when my friend was but five years of age, men dressed in suits and ties (fashion not often seen in the Minisink) parked a government-issued vehicle in the driveway of my friend's family's farm. Like several of my own ancestors, this family was made up of tenant farmers, those who worked someone else's land in exchange for a place to live and a cut of the harvest profits. Knowing why the men were there and what news they had come to deliver before they even opened their mouths, my friend's mother and father didn't bother to invite them inside, or even onto the porch. Instead, they stood, in the dirt driveway that overlooked the shallow yet wide river, and talked. They talked quietly so that the children in the house couldn't hear, but of course the children heard and one even rushed out, running to the arms of his mother with a face full of tears. It's the kind of thing, my friend told me, that you never forget as long as you live.

His family was told they had to leave. Te Army Corps of Engineers had arranged a settlement with the landowner: the house they lived in was to be razed, the land they farmed was to be inundated. They were told they had but days to pack and leave. If they didn't, if they resisted, they were told they would be forcibly removed. They were told, crushingly so, that the land wasn't even theirs to begin with. Their landlord would receive cash, and they, nothing. No assistance, no help finding a new home, nothing. They did not matter, to anyone, at all.

Their worst fears had turned into terrifying reality. Like everyone else who lived in the Minisink, they had listened to the rumors, watched the 1962 bill become law and the 1965 one expand upon it, all the while waiting, hoping, praying, that the men in the suits and ties wouldn't come to their door. But they did. And this is what the family was told: the government was going to build a dam across the Delaware at Tocks Island, to create a 30-mile long lake. More than 70,000 acres – an entire region – was to be submerged. The reason: flood control...or recreational possibilities...or electric power...or water supply – the reasons constantly changed and it depended upon who you asked, anyway. Reasons be damned, they said, the lake was coming. My friend and his family had to leave. So they did, fleeing to the plateau to the west.

But here's the thing. That land they used to farm? The land that was supposed to be flooded? It never was.

IV.

Almost two hundred years before the United States Congress doomed the Minisink, in the time when most North American colonists had stopped calling themselves British but legally still were, the (almost) white residents of the valley and the aborigines waged war on one another. The conflict was the direct result of the forced displacement of the Lenape from their ancestral homeland.

In what many consider one of the finest examples of British chicanery in the New World (or one of the earliest examples of American hustle, as a friend has pointed out), the sons of William Penn invented a claim to the territory surrounding the settlement of Wrightstown. Under pressure because they had already been illegally issuing tracts to settlers in the nearby Lehigh Valley, the Penns' agents told the Lenape leader that they rightfully owned as much land as could be travelled on foot, over the course of thirty-six hours, from the aforementioned town. So, in order to avoid open war with an opponent he knew was far more powerful, the leader agreed, thinking that the distance traveled in the specified direction (the west) wouldn't affect his people at all. He was very wrong.

The Penns hired three of the fastest and best-trained runners they could find. One of them ran two and a half marathons. 65 miles! When the cartographers finished their "calculations" the Penns claimed 1.2 million acres, including the land of the Minsi, the Lenape subgroup who lived between the western plateau and the eastern mountains. As is often the case in American history, what the white elite wanted, the white elite got.

They called on their native enforcers to make it so. Into the Minisink came the Six Nations of the Iroquois, the rulers and supposed protectorate of the Lenape people. Presented with an opportunity to expand their influence and political position, the former trading partner of the Minsi burned and murdered and pillaged their old friends (this statement is not meant to condemn the Iroquois, for all participants in this story have blood on their hands). Thousands and thousands of years of settlement and deeply planted roots meant nothing. The Lenape were told to leave. And so they did, for a while.

But they returned, and when they did, they did so violently. Over a ten year period, various Indian groups, including the displaced and furious Minsi, raided the white settlements of the Minisink. They used the tactics of what became known as guerrilla warfare: erratic strikes, sabotage, arson, and ambush. Wielding firearms and flaming arrows, the natives succeeded in ousting most of the descendants of the Hollanders and Anglo-Saxons from the region. If one word could be used to describe the atmosphere of this time, it would be terror.

By 1756, only five or so (almost) white families remained in the Pennsylvania portion of the region (including ancestors of my friend's family, who took shelter in Dupuy's fort, and steadfastly refused to leave as the Indians bombarded them). And while the war didn't reach their New Jerseyean counterparts on the other side of the river, many of those folks retreated to the more protected areas to the east of the mountains. Almost no one, Indian and white alike, remained.

If one word could be used to describe the story of the Minisink, it would be displacement.

V.

In the first half of the twentieth century, public works projects like the Tocks Island Dam were completed with little to no resistance. Environmentalism had yet to emerge as a dominant force in American politics, and the small rural communities threatened by these projects lacked the resources and the know-how to repel them. In particular, the Tennessee Valley Authority erected dam after dam in the South with relative impunity, displacing thousands and inundating countless acreage. As is often the case with these kinds of things, many of the local and state politicians involved in the TVA decisions lusted for the lakefront property that such inundation offered, hoping it would bring more wealth to their areas (and their own wallets, of course). This financial possibility was not lost on the people that initially supported the dam on the shallow river in the Valley of the Minisink.

The locals knew it. They knew. Ask anyone who remembers (there are fewer and fewer but they're still around), and they'll tell you: the politicians wanted lakefront property, that's what it was all about, flood control was but a ruse. As one woman told me, in a bar in the town of Milford, "those bastards, all they wanted was more and more money. They kicked us off of our land, saying they needed to control the flooding we all knew didn't need controlling. By the 1970s, the Army Corps of Engineers was talking about the need for additional recreation possibilities. Recreation? They took away my family's farm that had been in our family for almost two centuries, so rich people from New York City could sail fucking boats? Fuck them. Fuck. Them." Like my friend would say, it's the kind of thing you remember for the rest of your life, whether you're the teller or the listener.

Some locals held out, hoping the project would fail. But the government was tenacious. The laws had been passed. Who were they to object to the will of the American people? Some pointed out that senators from Oregon had no place deciding the fate of a region 3,000 miles away. But that didn't stop the men in the suits and ties from going house to house, farm to farm, to deliver the same painful news. And although they were "only doing their jobs," as someone involved told me, they still had blood on their hands.

Most agree that at least one suicide was tied to the Tocks evictions. Many think a second person took his life because of it, and others believe that the stress and grief of displacement claimed the lives of several more. I ask you: can you imagine the pain of being forced off your family's land, only to watch the federal government rent out the house your great-great grandfather built when the project hit delays? Can you?

I know I can. And it is unsurprising to me that a situation like this would end in death.

* * * * *

Even after they were displaced, after they bore the insult of watching their ancestral homes be occupied by others, and after more blood was spilled in the land between the plateau and the mountain, the inhabitants of the Minisink still resisted. In a remarkable display of human resilience, they fought the federal government of the United States of America, in order to preserve their valley. As the same woman told me that day in Milford, "It didn't matter that we couldn't live there anymore. It didn't. We still fought them tooth and nail. They told me once that they were going to dig up the cemeteries, and rebury all those people somewhere else. I remember thinking, you've got to be fucking kidding me. Thinking of them moving my father and mother...I wanted to throw up. I would have done anything to stop that dam from being built."

Others made appeals to the undiscovered history that would be lost. Forts from the French and Indian War, artifacts from the Lenape and their woodland ancestors, two of the best Paleo-Indian sites in all of America, all of these faced annihilation, they said. Still others made an argument based on beauty. As one literary production from the era declared, the region is "too beautiful to Inundate." Whether this was the river itself, the streams and creeks surrounding it, the eagle in the sky or the deer in the woods, the Minisink's exceptional beauty should matter, they argued. Others highlighted the dangers of government overreach, and broadcast their points of view in editorials, on news programs, and in the courts.

Soon, powerful media outlets like The New York Times and The Washington Post came out against the project. This rise in visibility, in turn, encouraged environmentalists from across the world to speak up, pleading for the preservation of the natural landscape. They hadn't been able to stop the dams from coming to the American South and West, but maybe, just maybe, they could stop this one. For them, the possibility of turning the Minisink into a wilderness utopia was nothing short of a dream, one worth fighting for, ardently. By this point, the political left and right had emerged as allies, and joined the moderates that had always opposed the dam, lending significant legitimacy to the anti-Tocks campaign. It wasn't long before those at the top joined the popular movement, and put an end to the project for good.

But while all of this resistance was building momentum, the locals faced another problem: what to do about the self-proclaimed "river people," the colony of hippies who had moved into the empty houses of the Minisink following the wave of evictions. They, too, are part of this story.

VI.

Some came from California, but the majority of the river people were from New York City. With the dam project facing delay, the Army Corps of Engineers sought to fill the vacant houses from which they had forced out the rightful occupants. In order to do so, they advertised in The Village Voice, the alternative weekly favored by the city's bohemian crowd. So, like the Dutch had done several centuries before them, hundreds of hippies headed from the former New Amsterdam to the valley between the plateau and the mountains.

These lovers of free love and an idolized nature saw in the Minisink an opportunity to finally realize a long-sought vision: a self-sustaining commune free from the trappings of postmodern life. So, while several did pay the federal government rent, more did not. A small army of squatters with violets and anemone in their hair had descended on the old river where the Paleo people, the Lenape, and the descendants of the Dutch and English had all once lived. In doing so, they became the latest (and the last, for now) wave of migrants this land has known.

There, they lived without electricity, hauling water from that vast river to their living quarters day after day after day. They drank homemade wine around huge bonfires, while some played instruments and others sang along, all of them trying to be free. During the warm days of spring and summer, they shed their clothes and bathed their naked bodies in the feather-like embrace of unadulterated nature. And, they did all of this with brains lit afire by substances that offered tantalizing glimpses at a world beyond reality.

So, in addition to tomatoes and squash, the river people grew marijuana and mushrooms in the cropfields that had once held chestnut trees, maize, and apple trees. Some of them even planted cannabis in the Minisink's cemeteries, and it became a new adornment to the sandstone graves of the Hollanders and Anglo-Saxons.

And, as might be imagined, these flower children earned the ire of those who had been displaced. I, once again, offer you the words of the woman from Milford: "You're asking about the hippies? The flower children or river people or whatever? Most of us hated them, yeah. It might not've been right, but we did. They were living in our houses! Growing pot in our graveyards! Squatting in our churches! That land was ours; it wasn't theirs. Uh-uh. No way. And, for whatever reason, they were the ones who got to live on it. Yeah, I guess it pissed us all off, big time."

There are stories of locals hurling abuses out of car windows, of nighttime raids when black-clad boys would make strange noises and bang on the houses with sticks, only to blend back into the deep and dark woods as the drunk river people staggered about, afraid. But the two groups never came to blows, and in a tribute to decency or progress or something, the Valley of the Minisink wasn't stained, once again, by human blood.

Even after the Army Corps of Engineers threatened them with bulldozers and the cops cracked down on their illegal farming practices, many of the squatters remained in the vacant houses. But eventually, their vision of a commune based on open love and worship of the land began to vanish. Some couldn't take the harsh living conditions (imagine living Amish-like but without the knowledge to do so), while others simply missed home. Still others longed for the promise of New York, preferring its human-authored beauty and ubiquitous motion to the quiet valley by the river. By the mid-1970s, almost all of them were gone.

But some of the river people chose to stay, for good. One such person was the best friend of my friend, the one whose family was told they had to leave their farm. And although I never met this man before he died, I've heard stories about him for years. He was one of the California hippies, a member of some of the original counterculture groups of the 1960s. Back before it was a fashionable thing for the wayward young to do, he had backpacked through Europe, combining day work with a little panhandling, moving from country to country, and meeting as many new people as he could. This was a man who also ate two or three or four mushrooms and then sunbathed nude on a scorching Pacific beach...for seven hours, with no sunscreen. He lived like this until one day, when he decided, on a whim, to travel across the American nation to the Pennsylvania-New Jersey border, so that he could live free and protest against the destruction of the environment. And unlike most of the friends he made there, he never left.

One summer, my friend and the hippie were partnered together on a grounds crew at a resort near Shawnee-on-Delaware, only two miles or so from Tocks Island. This was at a time after the river people had cleared out and the Minisink had been turned into a national park, when some people had begun to forget. My friend, who had once been evicted from a tract of land a few miles upriver, and the former squatter, who had once lived for free on the other side, worked the fertile floodplain ground of the resort. Together, they sent shovels and backhoe buckets into the earth, uncovering arrowheads and broken pieces of pottery and golf balls and other ghostly remnants of those who had come before. After work they'd stare at these totems and talk about the Indians or speculate about my friend's ancestors. Then, they would share a bottle of whiskey and a joint or two and talk about their deep, deep love of the land between the western plateau and the eastern mountains.

It is easy to see why they became friends. Forces set in motion many thousands of years ago had made it so.

VII.

The Valley of the Minisink is dead, but the land where it once was is now part of the Delaware Water Gap National Recreation Area. Millions of tourists travel there each year, but almost none of them know the story I have told you.

These residents of the east coast megalopolis drive their fifty miles on Interstate 80 to the water gap, retracing a route first forged hundreds of years ago. They park along the shallow yet wide river, pulling kayaks and canoes off their roofs, and seek adventure on the water that was almost dammed. They climb the mountain and walk that famous trail that would have been rerouted around a giant lake. They camp in the forests that would have been underwater, sitting around fires and partaking in the same revelries as the hippies who had once communed there. And, above all, these visitors close the gap between themselves and nonhuman nature in a land that has hosted human life for some twelve thousand years.

And despite everything that happened here, all the death and war and displacement and pain, I believe that there are far worse things the Minisink could have been turned into.

VIII.

But the Valley of the Minisink is dead and the afterlife I detailed in the previous paragraphs doesn't make this stark fact any less true. For places are uniquely human constructs: they are how we explain our relationships with the environments in which we live. If there are no people, there are no places. So when the federal government did what it did, when it evicted those who had lived between the plateau and the mountains for generations, it destroyed the Minisink forever.

I sometimes wish that the lake had been built, so that there existed at least some tangible, visible reason for why everything that happened, happened. I am not the only one who feels this way. Some longtime residents of the Poconos, the region of the western plateau, think the lake would have drawn away some of those who moved to the area in the '80s and '90s, when Monroe and Pike were the two fastest growing counties in the state of Pennsylvania. The influx of folks from New York and eastern New Jersey, they reason, might have stopped at the lake; in this utopic fantasy, the Poconos would have remained a rustic backwater and not become the latest exurb of the looming city at the end of the highway. But, I try to tell them, the lake would have had the opposite effect: the cost of land would have risen even higher than it did at the end of the twentieth century, and many of them might have lost their homes because of higher taxes and an elevated cost of living.

But the lake wasn't built, and people were displaced anyway. And we shouldn't withhold judgment about the cause, either: the indifference and incompetence of the American government, and the power and greed of those who constitute it, bear full responsibility for this tragedy.

It has never apologized for what it did. Not for unfairly displacing people for a project it never completed, not for filling those people's houses with others who had no claim to the land, not for the accompanying suicides, not for the decades of uncertainty and fear, not for anything. It never paid restitution or attempted to give back what it took or did anything to make the situation better for those who were affected. Instead, the elected officials and government employees of today throw up their hands at me and say, "at least there's a park." Like their counterparts back in the 1960s, they don't care, at all. Well, as my new friend from Milford would say, they can fuck off.

And therein lies one of the great lessons of this story. Many in America today misunderstand the distrust that large swathes of the population maintain toward government. Some cheekily assume it's because these folks don't know any better, or that they are manipulated into this mindset because of some lunatic on cable news, or that they want to do illegal things outside of the gaze of authority. In some cases, these might prove true, but in the land that surrounds what used to be the Minisink, a lot of people don't trust the government because that government did a very, very bad thing, and hurt lots of folks they knew. They are not crazy to fear that something like this will happen again. It very well could. Try explaining to them that it couldn't. They'll shut the door in your face.

When a place dies, especially in this completely preventable and stupid way, the effects are felt for generations. My cousin knows this from his experiences working for the aqueduct police, those who are charged with protecting the water supply of the City of New York. His primary area of coverage contains several large reservoirs located in the Catskill Mountains (if you were to follow the shallow yet wide river far enough upstream, you'd come to two of these). There, he encounters animosity from people who were told by their parents who were told by their parents about what his agency did around 1900, when it forced people out of their homes and burned down their churches because the big city needed drinking water. Over one hundred years later, he receives glares and silent threats. People have a way of remembering.

And those who used to live in the Minisink will tell their children about what happened, and those children will tell theirs, and so on, and so on. I hope that you, too, will remember this story of a place that once was, and tell it to as many people as you can. I hope we tell of it, forever.

The Fire Down Below: Centralia, Pennsylvania

For those to whom history is the presence
of ruins, there is a green nothing.
— Derek Walcott, Omeros

I.

They were strange-looking trees, the ones that formed the coal that ruined Centralia. They lived when the cone-ridden conifers began their life on Earth, back during the time of no flowers. In search of food from above, they grew to enormous heights, opening fern-like palms to sup rays of sunshine. High in the air, they formed unimaginable alien colonies, reproducing by the release of millions of microscopic spores.

But their ungainly height and shallow root systems made them prone to collapse. So they fell, one after the other after the other, on and on, for millions of years. On the muddy floors of Pangean swamps and river floodplains they rested, preserved by stagnant water and low populations of plant-consuming bacteria. There, they formed into a mucky mess with other plants and dead animals, until they were interred by sand or mud or some other sediment during massive, prehistoric floods. Their burial in the deep crust of the Earth was one of prodigious heat, which turned them into rocks like lignite, subbituminous coal, and bituminous coal.

Some of the swamps that once held the alien fern-trees, however, were subjected to the genesis of the Appalachian Mountains, back when they rose to be as tall as the Himalayas. The making of the great mountain chain of Eastern North America made these special rock deposits even hotter, and more serpentine, than their nearby counterparts. As a result, the coal that formed there was of another kind entirely: high-energy anthracite, the darling of the nineteenth-century American coal industry.

Over a stretch of time that's abstract enormity pushes against the human mind's ability to comprehend, the anthracite made its way from the equator to its present location in modern-day Pennsylvania. On the way there, the Himalayan-sized Appalachians wore down to nothing but a vast, flat plain. Then, around the time of the great extinction that heralded the demise of the dinosaurs and the rise of the mammals, the buried anthracite fields and the ancient bedrock that encased them rammed into hard volcanic rock, and were foisted upward yet again. From then until now, the watery forces of erosion have drained away the detritus to such a degree that the trees-turned-peat-turned-coal rest near the planet's surface, readily accessible to the hands of mankind.

It took the coal that ruined Centralia over 300 million years to form. But it only took one afternoon to light it on fire.

II.

I first visited Centralia, Pennsylvania in the spring of 2004. I was on a field trip for a college environmental geology class, and I was excited to see the destruction wrought by the famous underground coalseam fire. At the time I had little perspective on the town's tragic demise and the trauma inflicted upon its people. Instead, I was mostly concerned about whether or not I would see smoke rising from fissures in the ground. I longed to see melted asphalt and gaping sinkholes. I wanted to place my nineteen-year old hands on the earth and feel the hellish heat. In short, I was there for the spectacle.

Centralia did not disappoint. After riding south on PA-61 from the town of Sunbury for nearly 40 tortuous minutes, our van finally reached the limits of the destroyed town. We beheld a scene dominated by absence. A grid of paved roads intersected one another, but almost all of the formerly-occupied lots were vacant. Nothing but air remained where homes, businesses, churches, schools, and public halls once stood. "How is this even a ghost town," I said to the student seated next to me, "if there's nothing for the ghosts to haunt?"

The few buildings that remained had strange brick formations running from their roofs to the ground. Our professor explained that these structures helped support the walls of houses that had once been part of rowhomes. He said that some people still lived there, despite the fire down below. "Ten or twelve refused to leave," he said. "They won't last much longer. The government wants them gone. I'm surprised they managed to hold out this long." I gazed at those homes as we drove by, looking for signs of movement, signs of life. I saw none.

We parked by the graveyard. Placed high up on the edge of town, far from the ignited coal vein, the cemetery had escaped the fate that afflicted the rest of the community. Despite the annihilation surrounding it, the grounds were neatly mowed and bright plastic flowers decorated the gravestones of Centralia's dead. It was clear that someone still cared.

Turning away from the graveyard, our professor led us to a line of huge boulders that blocked off the stretch of Route 61 that was devastated by the fire. A sign met us. It read like a poem:

WARNING – DANGER

UNDERGROUND MINE FIRE

WALKING OR DRIVING IN THIS AREA

COULD RESULT IN SERIOUS INJURY OR DEATH

DANGEROUS GASES ARE PRESENT

GROUND IS PRONE TO SUDDEN COLLAPSE

We walked past the warning, and began to follow an anticlinal dip that plunged down the south face of Mahanoy Mountain. Two miles away and 600 feet below, the fishscale-shingled rooftops of the borough of Ashland were visible. "State geologists originally thought the fire would burn all the way to Ashland," our professor said as he pointed to the industrial town in the distance, "but it didn't go that way. We aren't sure why. But it did destroy this road."

He was right. An apt message composed of red spray-paint awaited us on the ghost road's cracked pavement. "Highway to Hell" it read, in gigantic, chthonic letters. We whispered to one another, the class more enticed than scared. I snapped photos with a bulky digital camera as my classmates explored the holes and cracks that dominated the terrain.

As we approached the part of the coalseam that was actively burning, the distinct scent of brimstone hit our nostrils. "Smells like rotten eggs," said someone close to me. "Sulphur," said another.

"Is it okay if we breathe this," my friend asked our professor. "Yeah," he responded. "Just don't stick your heads in the holes." We all thought of the toxic gases we had read about on the way in, but no one stopped.

We stepped over a rise and before us rose the sight we had come all that way to see: a hundred yards in the distance, smoke billowed out of a long, narrow crack in the road's surface. The heat of the fire had warped the road so much that the western side of the fissure was a full three feet above its eastern counterpart. Because of the potential danger, we never learned how far the hole in the ground went. Far enough, I thought.

"Coalseam fires are exceptionally rare," our professor said. "But when they happen, they create devastating environmental damage. A whole town was destroyed because of this event. Things like this will continue to happen until we finally pay enough attention to the heavy toll human activity takes on this planet. You all need to understand that when we destroy the environment, we destroy ourselves."

III.

If, as Sinclair believed, coal was king, then anthracite was God. Loaded with energy because of its special geological making, this so-called "hard coal" burns hotter, more efficiently, and cleaner than almost any other mineral found on earth. It is thus an exceedingly valuable resource, and man has lusted for it since at least the medieval period.

It was the Welsh (and possibly the Celts before them) that first pulled it from the ground and discovered its magical power. In America, an Englishman who had spent time in Wales noticed the similarity between Welsh rivers and the streams of the Pennsylvania colony, correctly deducing the presence of coal there. That was in

1698, over two-and-a-half centuries before the Centralia coalseam fire started.

But it wasn't until anthracite reached markets like New York and Philadelphia during the War of 1812 that demand for it began to grow. The warring British had halted shipment of Welsh coal to the Eastern Seaboard in the midst of the conflict, so many Americans were forced to find alternative fuel sources. Entrepreneurs from Pennsylvania exploited this opening in the war-time economy by selling their anthracite coal in the nation's major metropolitan areas. At first consumers were skeptical of the new fuel, but its sheer effectiveness stunned everyone who used it, homeowner and industrialist alike. Soon, people couldn't get enough of the hard coal from Pennsylvania, and anthracite joined whale-oil as one of the two most important fuels of the mid-nineteenth century.

The impact of the anthracite boom on the landscape, economy, and culture of the United States was colossal. In the mid-Atlantic states of Pennsylvania, New York, and New Jersey, construction and operation of coal-transportation networks like highways, canals, and railroads lifted entire regional populations out of rustic indigence. Some of these people were my very own ancestors, including my great-great-great-great grandfather who worked in a coal-fired iron furnace in New Jersey, my great-great-great-great-great uncle who worked for the Morris Canal, and my great-great grandfather who worked for a railroad company that freighted coal, iron, and other commodities to the bustling docks of Newark and Elizabeth. Coal was life-giving for my forbearers and for the millions of other poor Americans who toiled in the industry: it brought food to the table, good clothes for children, perhaps even a house on land you actually owned.

On the other hand, if you happened to be a wealthy turn-of-the-century New York socialite like the fictional advertising character

Phoebe Snow, you could take a ride on the anthracite-powered Lackawanna Railroad and go all the way from Manhattan to Buffalo. And, as the advertisements made clear, your beautiful white clothes, hair, and skin would stay impeccably clean during the entirety of your trip. As the ad brazenly bragged:

> Says Phoebe Snow
> about to go
> upon a trip to Buffalo
> "My gown stays white
> from morn till night
> Upon the Road of Anthracite."

From the lower classes that mined it to the wealthy train passengers whose clothes were unstained by it, anthracite had permanently changed the social fabric of American life.

It also unleashed seismic shifts in the ethnic composition of the nation, as countless European immigrants came to the United States seeking work in the coal industry. The impact of this great wave of migration was felt most forcefully in Pennsylvania. It is no coincidence that the decades in which anthracite hit its apex were the fasting growing in the state's history. The numbers are almost unimaginable: nearly 30% population growth for over half a century, three million new people, almost 40 new ethnic groups. And almost all of this change happened near the anthracite fields, which only comprise roughly 8% of the state's total area.

A whole new region was born. Town after town sprouted up, many with strange names like Alaska, Atlas, Strong, Ashland, and Centralia. Coal was the beating heart of all these places. But this turning of coal into gold was little more than modern alchemy. A horrible reckoning awaited.

IV.

Centralia was dying even before the coalseam fire started. Like many Rust Belt towns, it had fallen on hard times in the post-World War II era. Coal was still valuable, but its extraction was made significantly easier by the invention of mechanized mining technologies and more efficient removal techniques like strip mining. The days of the soot-covered Centralian miner, with his hard-hat, lantern, and lunch pail in hand, were pretty much over by the 1960s. The world had moved on.

This was a time of economic depression, one marked by a cavalier attitude toward the land. Indeed, with no centralized garbage disposal system available to them, residents of Centralia jettisoned their trash in illegal dumps located on the outskirts of town or burned it in their own backyards. They did so with little regard to issues of air quality, water-table contamination, and fire hazard. After all, the whole region owed its existence to environmental exploitation. How could its people be expected to care about land they were paid to savage, especially when their financial distress gave them little reason to care anyway?

Eventually, the town of Centralia arrived at a solution. A community landfill was constructed on the site of a foreclosed strip mining operation. It consisted of a huge pit, into which all of Centralia's waste was thrown. But soon the trash heaps piled high and the stench was too much and the town realized that it had to do something to clean up the mess. So instead of burying and subjecting the garbage to the same chemical processes of decomposition that created the coal located directly beneath it, the people in charge chose to burn it all instead. And while some still dispute the origin of the coalseam fire, it was undoubtedly this horrendously poor decision that started the blaze that went on to destroy the town.

At first, the townspeople did not realize the magnitude of the problem. But in August of 1962, some two months after the fire started, Pennsylvania mining officials detected deadly levels of carbon monoxide in a Centralia-area mine. The state acted immediately, shuttering all mining operations in the vicinity of the fire. At this point, several attempts were made to put it out and other forms of remediation also failed. The local, state, and federal governments decided to take a wait-and-see approach.

A year came and went, and nothing serious happened. And then another passed, and then another, until the fire had been burning for almost seventeen years with relatively little consequence. Predictably, fear of the blaze diminished. It became another part of life in the declining mining town. What the Centralians didn't realize, however, was that the fire was making its way to them like a slow-moving, subterranean snake. By 1980, it had slithered right beneath their feet.

Sinkholes opened up around town, including one that swallowed a child. Noxious fumes were released into the air wherever the land cracked from the pressure of underground heat. Anyone who breathed those gases was guaranteed a painful and immediate death. The local gas station owner worried that his tanks would turn into bombs and blow up half the town. The Centralia mine fire had gone from nuisance to existential threat. And there was no way to stop it.

V.

When I lived in southeastern Pennsylvania during my mid-to-late twenties, I sometimes drove through the Coal Region. Even if PA-61 was a slower route to my destination, I would often take it anyway. I did this because I wanted to see the declining towns. I wanted to soak in the mesmerizing aesthetic of rust that is rendered so evident there. I liked to stop and stare and think about what surrounded me. I tried to become an augur who could read the future of the American nation in the flattened mountain ridgelines and in the nervous paces of unemployed laborers.

I would go there because I wanted to know what it was like to live in a depressed region not all that far from my home. I wanted to see the remnants of the industry that my ancestors toiled in, to see the land that had given them – and me – life. But most of all, I went there because I wanted to know who chose to stay. And why.

On one such trip in 2010, I turned right at May's Drive-In in Ashland and began to ascend Mahanoy Mountain. I drove alongside the stretch of 61 that had been abandoned in 1994, where I had several years earlier seen the smoke of Centralia's coalseam fire. As I made a left to stay on the road and continue my way to Shamokin and then Sunbury and ultimately US-15N, I saw a handmade sign attached to a nonfunctional power pole. I pulled over so I could read it. Amazed by what it said, I took out my smartphone and shot a photo of it. It was another Centralian poem:

THESE RESIDENTS WANT
ABSOLUTELY NOTHING FROM
OUR GOVERNMENT, THEY
WANT TO LiVE WHERE
THEY CHOOSE !

PLEASE CALL –
Governor: Rendell 717-787-2500
717-787-5651   or 570-614-2040
Senator: Gardner – 717-787-8528
Rep: Belfanti – 570-339-5252

**AND DEMAND THAT THEY BE
ALLOWED TO REMAiN IN
CENTRALIA !!
THANK YOU!**

I was shocked. I stared at the words for a long, long time. My professor had been wrong, I realized. Some of the people he predicted would be forced out of their homes still lived in Centralia. I could not believe it: almost fifty years after the fire began, the final residents of the community still refused to leave their hometown.

VI.

By the mid-1980s, the situation in Centralia had reached a tipping point. There was near universal agreement that the town should be evacuated. But property owners were faced with an impossible dilemma: in order to move, they had to sell their homes or businesses, but these properties didn't have any value because they were located over an underground fire. There was much talk about what could be done. Would the state and federal governments step in? Would the people of Centralia be forgotten and overlooked, as they had been when coal went bust? Were they doomed to a literal living hell? It was not unreasonable of them to have had these thoughts. They had been left behind before.

The governments, however, did intervene. The Congress acted first, allocating over 40 million dollars for the relocation of the citizens of Centralia. Those that participated in the program were saved. They received far more money for their properties than they ever would have fetched on the open market, and they took that windfall and settled into nearby communities with relatively little difficulty. But, as is always the case whenever human beings are faced with the prospect of displacement, some Centralians resisted relocation. So they rejected the government's offer and stayed put.

The Commonwealth of Pennsylvania was not happy with this decision. This is not surprising, of course, since one of government's most sacred roles is the provision of security for its citizens. Pennsylvania's public officials considered Centralia to be unfit for human habitation, and they wanted the few people left there to move. So in the early 1990s, the governor of the state enacted eminent domain and condemned the town's remaining structures. But the people that still lived there took the issue to court.

They also created elephantine conspiracy theories. One claimed that Pennsylvania wanted their land so it could ultimately sell it to coal companies. The state could put out the fire if it really wanted to, they reasoned, but it let it burn so that it could displace them and reap profit from their lands. According to this narrative, the last Centralians saw themselves as the final bastion of resistance against a horrific incidence of government-driven displacement. They invoked examples from America's dark past, including the Tocks Island Dam Controversy, the Whiskey Rebellion, Indian Removal, the various projects of the Tennessee Valley Authority in the Southeast, and many others. They urged the American public to support their right "to live where they [chose]."

They also argued that the fire wasn't started by the landfill fiasco at all, that it was actually a continuation of another, nearby fire that had never been fully extinguished. They even suggested that maybe it had started on its own, a result of spontaneous combustion. "It wasn't us!" they desperately screamed, to all who would listen. And yet, underneath all of these myths one stark fact remained: the Centralians simply did not want to leave their hometown.

The disagreement between the two parties was full of acrimony, but it nevertheless spawned fascinating questions about the American nation and the rights of the people who live there. As a citizen of a liberal democracy, in which the dignity and freedom of the individual is fiercely championed and protected, can you choose to live in a dangerous place? Can the government forcefully remove you from your home? Can it displace you for your own safety, against your will?

By the time I read the handwritten sign in 2010, the last citizens of Centralia had managed to hang on for a quarter of a century. It should be noted that during their entire resistance, not a single remaining home fell into a sinkhole, no one breathed in fatal gas, and no fire-related injuries occurred. The dispute dragged into 2012, when the U.S. Third Circuit Court of Appeals denied the residents' last-ditch legal effort. Down to eight, but still doggedly determined, the group still refused to leave.

The issue was finally resolved the following year, when Pennsylvania officials agreed to let the remaining Centralians stay until their deaths, at which time their properties will transfer to the state. They got to stay. To this day, Centralia – population 6 – continues to survive.

VII.

The last time I visited Centralia was in the summer of 2014. I was with my wife, who was five-months pregnant with our first child, my father, my stepmother, and my eleven-year old brother. None of them had been there before, so I assumed the role played by my professor a decade earlier, explaining to them the story of this place and what had caused its death.

On the way there, I spoke of the formation of coal and the economic impact of the anthracite boom. I explained that, like me, my unborn child owed her life to the coal industry. We pondered the luck that results in the creation of human life, and we wondered if distant relatives of ours still lived in the Coal Region. Were the sloe-eyed young girls we saw walking the streets of Ashland our fourth, fifth, or even sixth cousins? Was it possible? Would we want to know? Did it even matter?

When we arrived in the space where the town had once been, we parked in the same place the college van had all those years before, right alongside Odd Fellows Cemetery. We walked through the streets that had no homes on them. We gazed at the few remaining houses and contemplated the decisions made by their occupants. We surmised that the word "home" had special meaning to them, one perhaps vastly different from our own.

And then we made our way to the abandoned stretch of PA-61, where I showed them why it is nicknamed "The Graffiti Road." Thousands of spray-painted messages blanketed the cracked highway. There were peoples' names, several demonic shapes, genitalia, and a few gorgeous, artistic renderings. There were images of dead animals and pink hearts and decapitated human heads. Symbols of love competed with messages of hate. All combined to form a chimerical, undecipherable text.

"Centralia is now a canvas for the world's wanderers," I said to my family. "Why don't you leave your mark?" I suggested to my little brother, pointing to a can of spray paint that sat on the edge of the road. He ran over, picked it up, and added his name to the ghost road. He then placed the can back where he had found it. "So someone else can use it next," he said.

He's right, too. They will keep coming to Centralia. And I hope that when they do, they will heed the lessons that can be learned there. I hope that they admire how hard people will fight for the right to live in their home place. I hope that they feel the gravity of a history that was some 300 million years in the making. But mostly, I hope that they learn to keep a careful eye out for human overreach and the environmental devastation it can sow.

As my family and I reached the top of Mahanoy Mountain, I stopped and pointed at the vacant streets. "This is what happens," I said, "when you destroy the environment. You destroy yourself."

The Place of Stone: Lapidum, Maryland

nothing but the blank faces of the houses
and cylindrical trees
bent, forked by preconception and accident–
split, furrowed, creased, mottled, stained–
secret

— William Carlos Williams, Paterson

I.

In February of 1899, a blast of Arctic air blanketed much of the United States, precipitating the fiercest winter in American history. It snowed on the beaches of the Gulf of Mexico. The ground froze for feet in the northern climes. The temperature reached -60 in Montana and even -2 in Florida. It was a devastating turn of events for a citizenry that was still some time away from achieving full electrification and the life-saving warmth it would provide.

But when the spring finally arrived, it brought another danger: ice dams. Because of the severe cold, massive ice accumulations had formed on many of the nation's frigid waterways. These glacial-like entities block riverflow, creating temporary reservoirs of water and ice. Although their creation is a natural and common event, ice dams are exceptionally hazardous to human life. After all, ice eventually melts, and when ice dams do succumb to the spring-time sun, they don't disappear gradually like their glacial brethren. Instead, they collapse catastrophically, and release torrents of water upon rivertowns unlucky enough to be located downstream.

This is what happened in the spring of 1899 on the mid-Atlantic region's biggest river, the Susquehanna. As the weather warmed, a series of ice dams on the upper stretches of the river collapsed, letting loose one of the worst frozen floods in American history. Millions of cubic feet of water laden with large chunks of ice moved down the river at a very rapid and dangerous rate of speed. It obliterated anything in its path, including homes, businesses, and lives. When it reached the settlement of Lapidum, a small town located near the head of the Chesapeake Bay in the state of Maryland, the flood had reached its maximum power and size. It breached Lapidum's limits and within seconds most of the town was gone.

But here's the thing that makes this story different: not a lot of people lived in Lapidum at the time of the frozen flood. The destroyed buildings were mostly unoccupied, thrown into disuse by economic headwinds stronger than a tidal wave of ice.

The ice dam's flood had destroyed nothing more than a ghost town.

II.

It is perhaps fitting that I don't recall how or why Lapidum was brought to my attention. Did I find it while driving around? Did someone hear of my interest in lost places and tell me about it? Did I Google "ghost towns near me" and it popped up? I truly don't remember. Like much about the town itself, Lapidum's entry into my orbit remains a mystery.

I do, however, remember my first visit. After driving over one of Interstate 95's longest bridges, I exited and made my way into the gorge carved out by the Susquehanna. It was a steep and narrow descent, but eventually the terrain opened up and I found myself facing the big river. To my left were some stone ruins, to my right was an unused boat launch.

I parked the car and got out. It was a cold February day, so there was no one else around. I was the only ghost in town.

The first thing I noticed was a rectangular-shaped hole filled with frozen, swampy water. I later came to learn that this had been Lock 9 of the Tidewater Canal, an important piece of infrastructure that helped sustain Lapidum during the nineteenth century. Beyond the lock lay the snow-covered remains of a railroad track. Ensnared by vines and covered by a century's worth of detritus, this artifact of a bygone era of industrial production was in the process of being reclaimed by the natural world.

I moved from the lock toward the stone ruins I had seen on the way in. The set closest to my car was the foundation of a relatively small building. Because of its distance from the river, proximity to the lock, and the presence of a crumbled chimney on its western side, I assumed that it had once been a human dwelling, perhaps a lock-keeper's residence. But there was no evidence of its former occupants.

As I made my way toward the Susquehanna, I tried to imagine the former town and found, troublingly, that I could not. It was too far gone and my mind couldn't find a way to reconstruct it. Nothing but inchoate, fleeting images ran through my head.

A little while later, I came to the biggest group of ruins: three square foundations pressed up against each other on a hill overlooking the river. A faded historical marker announced that I was gazing at the remains of the Susquehanna Hotel, a former resting point for weary travelers, and, later, a place of repose for men from

Baltimore who longed to escape the sooty drudgery of the urban world. The sign also stated that the Hotel existed until the 1960s, long after the rest of Lapidum had disappeared. But even it had been gone for half a century by the time I first saw it.

Part of the former hotel's foundation had given way in a landslide of mud, metal, and earthenware. I walked up and took a closer look. Several pieces of broken pottery laid half-buried in the ground. Some of them were gorgeously inlaid with azure lines – evidence of the popular blue willow style favored by the upper classes of the 1800s. Others were thick and mundanely-glazed, the kind used in old piping. Here, I thought at last, is something besides stone piles. People did live here – and when they broke their plates and bowls, they buried the rubbish in a hole in the basement. Now, their discarded garbage awaits whoever chances upon it.

I found a last clue of human presence behind the site of the former inn. Cut deep into the mountainside were huge gaps. These quarries were what gave the town its name: Lapidum, the place of stone. Quartzite the color of dirty alabaster was strewn throughout them. This especially strong and dense rock, painstakingly removed from the hills around town by non-mechanized manual labor, was originally used by the townspeople to build their homes and other structures. Eventually they began exporting it, using the interlocking ferry and canal network to ship it across America.

Masons took stone from the Lapidum area and made forts and courthouses and manors and prisons and tunnels; quite literally, the little town's rocks formed the foundations of a rapidly-growing nation.

But despite this evocative fact, things change and ice melts.

III.

The first humans to come to the land that would become Lapidum were the Paleo-Indians. Asiatic in ethnicity, these people followed bison and mammoths and other megafauna across the ice bridge that formed on the Bering Strait during the most recent Ice Age. Some went south, following the Pacific Coast into modern day California. Others, though, headed east along the southern tip of the huge Wisconsin glacier. Study of their material culture and bones suggests that bands of Amerinds reached the banks of the Susquehanna as early as 11,000 BCE. Some experts suspect they were there even earlier.

Living in a time of scarcity without the benefits of agriculture or medicine, these people left little behind. What they did cast off lays buried beneath thousands of years of soil and sand. Aside from their propensity for making long, thin, and strong arrowheads known as Clovis points, we know little about them.

But as enigmatic as the Paleos might seem from an archaeological standpoint, there is one key fact that can help us understand them: they were anatomically-modern humans, just like us. That means they had the same brains, the same bodies, and the same behaviors. They formed communities and utilized technology to survive. They also experienced the full range of human emotion and affect. Disappointment, sadness, joy, love, hate, pain, hunger, grief, thirst, lust, anger, fear, triumph – all these are ours, and thus, they were theirs, too.

It is not difficult to imagine what they were like. Picture them encamped along the Susquehanna, a fire keeping the glacial wind at bay. Maybe they ate nuts or fish or meat from some otherworldly animal they had killed. Being humans, it is without doubt that they told stories while they dined, tales perhaps inseparable from their cosmology. If there were children, they likely danced and sang and wrestled in the mud while the adults cheered and clapped.

And, like us, they died – from disease, from infection, from injury, from poison, from the attacks of other humans. But being people, they buried their dead, performing rituals probably not all that different from the funeral rites administered around the globe today.

Eventually, however, the Paleo people left the place of stone, taking with them their many mysteries. But what had attracted them to that place was the same thing that had attracted the first European settlers: the Susquehanna River.

IV.

John Smith explored the entire Chesapeake Bay in 1608, over a decade before the Pilgrims and their Mayflower reached Plymouth. Edward Palmer set up a trading post on an island in the middle of the Susquehanna's mouth in 1622. Nearby Havre de Grace was founded in 1658. In 1683, land grants were issued for what would ultimately become Lapidum. All of these early white people coveted the Susquehanna.

Like the Delaware that flows through what used to be the Valley of the Minisink, the Susquehanna River is one of the oldest continuously flowing streams in the entire world. In fact, only one large river is of more advanced age: the Finke that drains central Australia. But even the Finke's flow is interrupted by prolonged periods of drought. Only the Susquehanna has flowed unabated for nearly 325 million years. It is so old that it predates the very ocean it runs into.

It is quite long, too. Beginning at Ostego Lake in Cooperstown, New York, the Susquehanna flows for over 450 miles. Along the way, it slices through the ridgelines of the Appalachian Mountains, forming several dynamic water gaps. As these beautiful geological formations suggest, not even erosion-resistant sandstone can withstand the river's force. In fact, it took a meteor strike to form the Chesapeake Bay itself. Without intervention from the cosmos, the Susquehanna would have continued to pour into the Atlantic Ocean until another ocean took its place. But the immense hole created by the impact event turned the lower portion of the river into a ria – a flooded ancient riverbed – that went on to become America's largest bay.

Neither the Paleo people nor the white settlers knew these important and determinative geological facts. Instead, what drew them to the river were quintessential human desires: freely available food, fertile farmland, and easy navigation up and down the Bay.

The fish were the biggest draw. The Susquehanna has over 60 native species, including the American shad, a particularly fecund type of herring. These migratory animals appear only for a few days a year, when they head upstream to reproduce and complete their life-cycle. They are so outrageously numerous, however, that communities like Lapidum could net enough fish to last all year long – with plenty to spare for exporting.

While the fishing industry helped eighteenth-century Lapidum develop into a busy little river community, the town's strategic location was what really made it prosper. For instance, the establishment of the nearby Upper Ferry allowed travelers to move across the Susquehanna to the other side, where the states of Delaware and Pennsylvania could be conveniently accessed. Before crossing, these people stayed in Lapidum, injecting capital into the local economy.

In the early nineteenth-century, the Tidewater Canal opened up the Susquehanna itself – strewn with devastating rocks that caused John Smith to turn around only a few miles upstream from the Bay, the river cannot accommodate large ships. The Canal, though, enabled goods to be shipped to the Chesapeake region from as far away as Lake Erie and parts of upstate New York. As one of the northernmost deepwater ports near the Bay, Lapidum was the site of the aforementioned Lock 9.

Commodities like iron ore, wheat, tobacco, fish, coal, flint, marble, quartzite, corn, and many others flowed through town. Amid all of this success, the population grew to a respectable size. By the middle of the nineteenth century, Lapidum had a few hundred residents, a school, a church, and even its own Masonic Hall – fitting, of course, for the place of stone. But it wasn't destined to last.

V.

The town's decline was instigated by what the great naturalist writer Frank Norris once called the octopus: the major railroad conglomerate. In the case of Lapidum, it was the Baltimore and Ohio Rail Road Company – otherwise known by its Monopoly moniker, the B&O.

The battle between the Tidewater Canal and the B&O was overwhelmingly won by the railroad. For one thing, canal traffic was quite slow. By the time a barge was raised or lowered on a lock, a train could have traveled several miles. Trains also required less physical labor. Imagine mules and leggers and bargemen and slaves dragging heavily loaded barges up and down hundreds of miles of canalways. Contrast this with the B&O engineer sitting in his powerful steam engine, hauling vastly more goods in a fraction of the time. The B&O was bigger, better, and faster, so it won. It also bypassed Lapidum, leaving the town cut off from the only serious economic force in the region.

Thus ended the mercurial canal upon which Lapidum depended. The ferries that brought travelers into town also faded from use and were replaced by passenger rail. No one needed Lapidum stone anymore, either; the nation was hungry for steel, not rock. Even the fish had stopped coming in their previous numbers. Though the people of the era did not recognize it at the time, the fish populations of the Chesapeake had been gravely wounded by overharvesting. In addition, the pollution dumped in the Susquehanna's watershed during the industrial revolution had significantly deteriorated the Bay's various ecosystems.

In the face of this decline, Lapidum's people moved to the growing metropolises of Baltimore, Wilmington, and Philadelphia. Following the ice dam's flood in 1899 and a subsequent one in 1904, only one building remained in the former town: the Susquehanna Hotel.

VI.

The Hotel was magnificent. Its builders designed it before the Queen Anne architectural movement, so it took on a more classical Victorian appearance: short sloped roofs, large covered porches on the front and back, dual chimneys, stone and brick foundations visibly apparent on the bottom floor, and pinned down ornamental shutters adorned to its many windows.

What had once been a place of rest for those seeking crossing into the northern states in the mid-nineteenth century had become a place of sport for rich white men by the 1910s. The rise of white-collar positions in large companies had given birth to a new leisure class, and these wealthy urbanites lusted for experiences outside of their offices and cities. No doubt inspired by the projection of rugged masculinity exuded by Teddy Roosevelt in the century's opening decade, men came to Lapidum to fish in the Susquehanna, to hunt waterfowl nesting near the big river and its tributaries, and to shoot deer, fox, rabbits, squirrels, and bear in the fallow fields that had once grown tobacco and corn.

So the Susquehanna Hotel entered a new section of the post-bellum American economy: sporting tourism. Hunting and fishing lodges had begun appearing up and down the Eastern Seaboard around the turn of the century, most located within a day's travel of America's largest cities. To the north, New Yorkers rode the Delaware and Lackawanna Railroad to the Delaware Water Gap, where they took stagecoaches into the wilderness of the Pocono Mountains. There, they sought the fish known variously as the hemlock, speckled, or brook trout – the Appalachian Mountains' only native salmonid. Others ventured to the Catskills, as far back as when the region was still spelled Kaatskill, and tried out the newest fashionable sport for upper-class businessmen: fly fishing.

In the mid-Atlantic, people from Washington and Baltimore were drawn to resorts located on the Chesapeake's Eastern Shore. While the men sought rockfish and other quarry, their wives and children enjoyed crabbing, tennis, and sunbathing. Some of the families even summered there, with the men traveling back and forth to work each week. It was this growing regional industry that kept the last remaining business in Lapidum going for the first half of the twentieth century.

The Hotel held on until the 1960s. By that point, automobiles and airplanes had made travel to more exotic and interesting locales far easier. Why travel to the shores of the Susquehanna when you could hop on a plane and end up on the banks of the Seine or the Thames or the Rhone? Why cast for rockfish when you could drive on Route 66 to the American West and access the famed trout streams of Yellowstone? Why boat on the Chesapeake Bay when you could sail around the warm and lush Florida Keys?

Furthermore, the Philadelphia Electric Company had erected a hydroelectric dam on the big river four miles upstream from the

Hotel in 1928. This enormous structure cemented the ecological damage begun in the 1800s, and, as a result, put the sporting lodge out of business.

VII.

When Popular Science Monthly wrote about the Conowingo Dam in 1930, the hydroelectric power plant already held several distinctions. It was the second most powerful operation of its kind in the whole world, possessed the largest circuit-breaking switches ever made, and was controlled by a network of incredibly sophisticated switchboards. The magazine lauded the project, calling it an example of American "Progress and Discovery."

At the time, people saw the dam as a symbol of national achievement. It was evidence that America's technologically-advanced society could conquer something as imposing as the nation's wild landscape. Conowingo was proof that America was still moving forward, that it was still capable of doing great things. Given the uncertainty in the air following the market crash of the previous October, this attitude made a lot of sense to a lot of people.

But few thought of the consequences. As the example of the proposed Tocks Island Dam shows, even the mere idea of a dam's construction causes chaos and suffering. Unlike that situation, Conowingo happened. It was built.

To make way for the dam, the settlement of Conowingo was displaced. Its people could not overcome the will of the power company or the federal agencies who saw the dam as a national necessity. So Conowingo's people were moved from their homes in the name of progress and discovery. Whatever remains of that place rests well below the surface of the dam's reservoir.

As awful as the displacement of the Conowingo residents was, the environmental damage caused by the dam was even worse. To begin, the hydro plant was a cataclysm for the fish that had lured the white settlers to the head of the Bay. Shad, like many other herring, are nomadic by nature; any impoundment in their path can severely disrupt their lifecycle. It so happened that the Conowingo Dam was built only ten miles from the mouth of the river. Shad were used to swimming hundreds of miles upstream. And for decades, Conowingo blocked their way. Today, the shad are aided by fish ladders that, while helpful, cannot adequately address the severity of the problem. Fish biologists believe that the Susquehanna's American shad population has been reduced by 50%.

Another significant problem has developed because of sediment blockage. Indeed, lurking beneath the lake created by the dam is a massive pile of phosphorous, soil, and miscellaneous chemicals – decades worth of runoff from the farms and parking lots and suburban yards and city streets located upstream.

It is a problem of monumental proportions. Over 25,000 square miles of land drain into the Susquehanna watershed. This happens literally every second of every day, as it has for hundreds of millions of years. But the construction of the Conowingo Dam halted the natural flow and distribution of the water and its sediments. When the affluvion hit the wall of the dam that first day in 1928, it had nowhere to go. The gigantic pile was started.

The problem was further exacerbated by flood control measures implemented by streamside cities like Sunbury, Harrisburg, and Northumberland. While levees helped save places like these from the devastating effects of flooding, they have also kept millions of tons of sediment in the river that would have otherwise spilled onto the Susquehanna's floodplains. Instead, all of that material makes its way to Conowingo. Before long, a century's worth of sediment will be pressed up against the aging structure. Government experts predict the reservoir will reach its holding capacity in 15-20 years. What will happen then? No one seems to know.

In the meantime, if a powerful tropical system were to deal the region a direct blow, there might not be anything the operators of the dam could do: much, if not all, of the deadly pile would be released into the Chesapeake Bay, poisoning it beyond all reckoning. It would be an extinction-level event for many of the Bay's plant and animal species – and for the towns and cities that rely on them for their economic livelihoods.

If this were to happen, if the mountainous pile of submerged dirt were set loose from its moorings, the ruins of Lapidum would be buried much like the town was once buried by a wave of ice.

VIII.

The land that Lapidum used to rest on is now part of the Susquehanna State Park – a beautiful strip of protected land on the west bank of the river. Like the former Valley of the Minisink, this lost place has become a site for recreation and conservation.

It was a warm day in the month of May the last time I visited. I took some photographs, chatted with some anglers and bird-hunters, and searched for signs of life amongst the ruins. On the way out, I decided to take the dirt road that cuts northwest along the big river. After a few minutes of driving, a huge bird flew over the car and into the overhead canopy. It was a bald eagle.

In these post-Silent Spring days, the sighting of an eagle near the lower Susquehanna is a commonplace occurrence. The base of the Conowingo Dam, it turns out, is a favorite feeding ground of America's national bird. An opportunistic predator, the eagle has discovered that Conowingo blocks fish from swimming upstream. The bird also realized that the powerful discharge releases from the dam prevent the water from freezing in the colder months. So, every November and December, hundreds of eagles descend upon the Conowingo Dam, where they feast on trapped herring or perch or bass until spring.

And hundreds of human beings flock to them. Drawn for the spectacle – or for the photographic prospects – these people line up underneath the mammoth dam and watch the eagles. Sometimes the birds wash their feathers in the water. Sometimes older, larger eagles wait in streamside trees until adolescents catch fish, and then bombard them in the air and steal the younger birds' prey. Sometimes they simply soar, not flapping their wings for what seems like impossible amounts of time. Often, the eagles don't do anything. But the birdwatchers are always ready with their cameras in case they do.

This is what Lapidum and its environs have become: a place for the American people to watch eagles, catch fish, photograph wildflowers, or shoot ducks. Of course, a town used to be there, and it is not anymore. But the place where it once stood has reverted back to a more primal state, where people do what people have done since they began coming to the banks of the Susquehanna all those millennia ago: engage with the natural world on their own terms.

The Broken Region: The Copper Basin

Trees are like men, differing widely in character; in sheltered spots, or under the influence of culture, they show few contrasting points; peculiarities are pruned and trained away, until there is a general resemblance. But in exposed situations, wild and uncultivated, battling with the elements and with one another for the possession of a morsel of soil, or a favoring rock to which they may cling-they exhibit striking peculiarities, and sometimes grand originality.

— Thomas Cole, "Essay on American Scenery"

I.

Barren red hills were once the dominant feature of the Copper Basin, a geological formation that encompasses parts of southeast Tennessee, northwest Georgia, and far southwestern North Carolina. This region's treeless, denuded landscape was the result of contamination from its many sulfuric acid manufactories. For decades, poison spewed forth from their smokestacks and smothered the surrounding area. Eventually, most local plant life died.

By the time of the Great Depression, a Dust-Bowlian moonscape was what the residents of the Copper Basin called home. The ubiquity of the redness sowed within these Americans an unbalanced sentiment that was at once somber and prideful. Yes, their home had been scarred by an intense ecological disaster, but the act of scarring had gifted them a unique and special scenery. It was theirs. It was home.

Unmarked by the green of healthy nature, the sterile hills became a symbol of their local identity; that is, until the land was successfully remediated in the mid-to-late twentieth century. Today, long-time residents of the Copper Basin nostalgically yearn for the time when their red hills still covered the land, when as children they rode sleds down the dusty hillsides and burrowed holes into the soft chalky earth.

Indeed, the people of this place are not fully at peace with the success of the environmental remediation. They feel like it took something – something close, deep, and pure – from them.

I know what this is like. The region where I am from, the Pocono Mountains of Pennsylvania, has seen tremendous change throughout the last century. What was once a hotspot tourist destination for the wealthy of New York City and Philadelphia has seen many of its once sprawling, all-inclusive resorts fall into ruin. And nature has rapidly reclaimed them. On the old golf courses small trees and invasive plants battle for the open space. Meanwhile, through the broken windows of old luxury hotels, vines snake their way in and set their roots on the decaying wood floorboards. This is hard for me to look at, having witnessed firsthand the economic devastation that this regrowth signals.

As someone who has championed the conservation and preservation of the American land for my entire life, I tell myself that I should come to terms with the decline of my home area's tourism industry and the coterminous collapse of its subprime-loan fueled housing market. Nature has clearly benefitted from both. But I don't feel that way. Instead, like the residents of the Copper Basin, I feel deep and guttural sensations of grief toward these undeniably positive ecological outcomes.

From the outside looking in, these sentiments might seem preposterous. How could anyone have nostalgia for environmental degradation? But see, American regions like the Poconos and the Copper Basin have been swept up in a whirlwind of economic and social change. This deeply affects the way people view things. And it should.

Copper Basin residents have seen their red hills disappear along with their copper industry, they have been witness to violent political upheaval that threatened the peaceful way of life that had been their hallmark and pride, they have been rocked by a scandal centered on an illegal abortion and adoption ring, and they continue to watch helplessly as their area slips further into an economic and cultural malaise fueled in no small part by a rampant opioid addiction epidemic.

Like the Poconos I once knew, the place of the simple red hills is gone. It is lost. It cannot and will not be restored. What is left is a matrix of sadness and fear and pain, without much hope for the future.

II.

I had driven through the Copper Basin in the fall of 2014, but it was not brought to my full attention until the spring of 2016, when an alumnus of my institution heard about my work on lost places and told my wife about his hometown of Copperhill.

Copperhill, Tennessee and McCaysville, Georgia should, by all accounts, be part of the same town: their sidewalks flow into one another, the storefronts are lined up in quick succession, and the road that runs through them is uninterrupted. They are divided, however, by a state boundary, which cuts diagonally through the communities. It is marked by a painted blue line and people sometimes pose for photographs with one foot in one state and one foot in the other. It is an arbitrary feature of division and fracture that is a perfect metaphor for this place.

Along with the nearby community of Ducktown, TN, the Copperhill/McCaysville mashup operates as something of an unofficial capital of the region.

It is a strange place.

The odd blue line notwithstanding, the two adjacent towns offer stark experiences...depending on when you happen to be there. If you were to wander your way into the town(s) in the middle of the week or in the dead of winter, you'd find hardly a business open, save for the IGA grocery store and the too-crazy-to-be-true dual pharmacy and firearms retailer, Drug and Gun. Come back on a warm weekend or a crisp fall day, however, and you'd see hundreds of people walking the streets, popping into restaurants, and buying stuff at antique shops and boutiques.

Adorned with circular stickers marking them as paying customers, this flood of humanity is sometimes referred to as "the train people" by residents of the Copper Basin. Indeed, they do come by train, all thirteen miles from the town of Blue Ridge, Georgia on the touristy Blue Ridge Scenic Railway. Most of the train people are out-of-towners, many of whom drive up from the Atlanta metropolitan area to experience the good old days of passenger rail in the rural United States.

As part of their trip, the train people are treated to an hour's repose in what the operation describes as the "quaint sister towns of McCaysville, Georgia and Copperhill, Tennessee." And when they are there, the place is, in fact, quite quaint: many of the town(s)'s businesses are only open during the hours when the train people come.

But it's when the train people are gone that the real, lost Copper Basin creeps forth from the shadows. I have seen addicts lined on curbs, shady transactions in empty parking lots, and too-thin people squatting in the brick-strewn shambles of crumbled buildings. I've seen the barbed-wire fences that prevent people from walking through the regrown red hills and accidentally falling into old mine shafts. And I've seen up close the forlorn factories and the polluted containment ponds that rest as silent monuments to the industry that both gave and took from the surrounding communities.

This division, this strange contrast, between the train people days and the ghost people nights, is nothing short of terrifying. The train is quite literally life support for a dying place. Should it ever stop rolling down the tracks, the Copperhill/McCaysville dyad won't just suffer – it'll disappear forever.

III.

As is the case with most North American places, the Paleo peoples were the first residents of what ultimately became known as the Copper Basin. Around 12,000 years ago, the area offered these hungry humans a vast array of natural resources: its lush, verdant forests provided plenty of game and vegetables, while its ancient rivers offered clean water and fish and freshwater clams. These nomadic tribes eventually left the Basin for places unknowable to contemporary man, leaving nothing behind but a phantom-like whisper of their presence.

The Amerinds were followed by participants in the Woodland period, the time in which the native peoples transitioned from spears and clubs to bows and arrows. Like their pre-Columbian ancestors, the Woodlanders moved in and out of the Basin for centuries; however, it wasn't until the ascent of the Mississippian culture around 1000 CE that the Copper Basin finally hosted permanent human settlements.

The Mississippians are perhaps best known for the series of earthen burial mounds they erected throughout the southern United States (they are also the subject of this book's eighth chapter). Although their mounds are glorious architectural achievements that have lasted to the present day, the Mississippi people's greatest innovation was undoubtedly agriculture. It was they who brought maize to the Basin, clearing fields out of the towering forests with controlled blazes and the labor of their own muscle. They lived this way for hundreds of years, until white Europeans made contact with them and brought their society to a state of collapse. The addition of smallpox and typhoid into their communities was what cemented their decline.

Into the void left by the destruction of the Mississippi culture came the Cherokee, the tribe to which the Copper Basin still maintains the most direct and meaningful connection. They came from the north, settling into the spaces already cleared by those who came before them. And although the Cherokee spread throughout the Basin, they maintained a significant village near the edge of today's Copperhill, right at the confluence of Fightingtown Creek and the Ocoee River.

There, they found the rock that gives the region its name.

IV.

Long before humans learned the godlike capacities of iron, they made weapons and art and tools from copper. This moment in humanity's development is sometimes known as the Chalcolithic period, a time in which the earliest human civilizations start to appear in the historical record. This is certainly not a coincidence.

The control of copper led to improvements in almost every avenue of human life. Wherever it was found – in Turkey, in Serbia, around the Great Lakes of North America – it was put to immediate and heavy use. And, given the violent nature of human nature, those early peoples that found copper used it to produce deadlier weapons and stronger armor than had hitherto been seen.

In Europe, copper axe heads were such a significant technological advantage in warfare that anthropologists believe they gave birth to an entire European ethno-group called the Corded Ware culture. Their success was tied to their metal weapons; and, to this day, residents of northern and Western Europe contain these ancient peoples' genetic legacy. One could make an argument that the development of copper-based technologies in Europe produced the Western World as we have come to know it.

Back in the Copper Basin, the Cherokee used the region's copper deposits to make tools and, of course, armaments. Once white settlers arrived in the region during the early nineteenth century, they "discovered" copper instead of gold, resulting in what we may label a "copper rush" to the area. Ever since then, the people of the Copper Basin have been producing copper-derived commodities. It should be noted, again, that the sulfuric acid that destroyed the area's vegetation was one of these products.

But today, in 2017, almost all of the region's copper mines and factories have shut down. The consequences of the area's economic collapse in the 1950s and 1960s was wide-ranging and disastrous.

V.

While conducting research for this essay, I came across a private Facebook group devoted to preserving the pictorial history of the Copper Basin. I asked to join, and my request was granted. I periodically checked on the group to see if any new photos appeared, so that I might gain a deeper understanding of this lost

place and its history; however, a post one day grabbed my immediate attention. It was a woman asking for any information about
an illegal adoption ring that was run by a doctor named Thomas
Hicks. The woman's name was Priscilla, and she turned out to be
one of the so-called Hicks Babies – a group of over 100 people
who were sold out of the backdoor of Hicks' McCaysville clinic
during the 1950s and 1960s. I had to know more.

I contacted Priscilla with a Facebook message explaining who
I was, what I work on, and why I was interested in her story. To my
delight and surprise, she answered quickly and we set up a phone
interview. We spoke for over two hours about her experiences as
a Hicks Baby, about what it was like to search for her origins over
the course of a lifetime, and about her ambivalent feelings toward
her hometown/not-hometown. At that point, she invited me to
join her and two other Hicks Babies during an upcoming trip to
the Copper Basin.

I met Priscilla, Emily, and Louise on a way-too-hot, humid southern day in the parking lot of the IGA in downtown
Copperhill. I was astonished to learn that this was Emily's first trip
back to the place of her birth since she was passed out the back
window of Hicks' clinic to a desperate couple from Ohio. As the
group walked to the building where Hicks committed his crimes,
an amalgam of emotions came over me: fear, awe, pity, love, anger
– you name it, I felt it then.

I watched as Emily stood by the threshold from which she was
once passed (trafficked, we might even say). Although I had only
known them for about half an hour, I teared up with the rest of
them. I could see the terrible weight of history and pain on Emily's
face. I've never seen anything quite like it.

We ended up in the home of a ninety year old woman named
Doris, a person who knew Dr. Hicks and his family. She claimed to
also know the identities of several of the Hicks Baby birthmothers,

but swore she would take their secrets to her grave. In many ways, Doris has become a mother herself to the Hicks Babies. Deep love exists between them.

According to Doris and to my own informed opinion about the region's history, Dr. Hicks was motivated in part by the economic decline of the Copper Basin. With depression comes a myriad of social issues, including rising rates of unwanted pregnancies, drug use, etc. For better or worse, Hicks took matters into his own hands during an era when his region was beginning to fall apart, abortion was illegal nationwide, and women were prevented from adopting children if they had a previous divorce or any minor criminal background. As some of the Hicks Babies claim, Thomas was "ahead of his time" in that regard.

Nevertheless, Dr. Hicks unleashed some serious demons. Like Goethe's Faust, the town doctor had indeed entered into a deal with the devil. He kept no records of who birthed the children. He forged birth certificates. He wrote prescriptions for drugs that people were addicted to. When one toys with life and death in these ways, Mephistopheles always comes calling. And he usually wants blood.

Hicks was caught performing an illegal abortion, was arrested, and stripped of his medical license. He retired, and possibly lived off of the money he made selling children. When he died, he took with him all knowledge of his adoption ring. For the Hicks Babies, there seemed to be no hope of ever finding their birth parents.

I told this to Priscilla, Emily, and Louise. I told them it was my belief that too much time had gone by – most of their birth parents were likely dead. And if they were still alive, they very much may want to have their terrible secret never come to light. I did, however, offer them assistance in the only way I could: I wrote an essay documenting their experiences and published it with the literary magazine Narratively. I emphasized to them the importance of finding new audiences for their story.

I, however, kept my overall pessimism regarding the discovery of any birth parents, the holy grail for the Hicks Babies. The odds were heavily – heavily! – stacked against them. I maintained this attitude for almost a year.

But then I got a shocking note from Emily: she had found her birth mother.

Despite the destruction of records and despite the death of Hicks and despite the silence of Doris, there was still a way to solve the mystery. It was right with the Hicks Babies the whole time, running through their veins, hiding beneath their very skin. In what can only be described as tremendous irony given the role that acid played in the destruction of the Copper Basin's ecology, a different kind of acid revealed Emily's origins: deoxyribonucleic acid, or, as it is popularly known, DNA.

And although her birth father was long since dead, Emily's biological mother was still alive. They were reunited two weeks previous to the writing of these words.

In Emily's note, she thanked me for helping her on her journey. And even though my essay wasn't the reason she found her mother, in Emily's eyes all who assisted her in the quest to unlock her life's biggest mystery deserved credit. I did not, and do not, feel worthy of this or of her admiration. Nevertheless, those were some of the most powerful words someone has ever sent me.

Late that night, I laid in bed, unable to sleep. Images of the Copper Basin kept flashing through my mind, with the look on Emily's face as she stood outside the former Hicks clinic appearing and reappearing every few seconds. Overcome with emotion, I cried.

I turned to my wife and told her how this is a terrible world we live in. Bad things happen to good people every single day.

And no place thrusts that reality into such exquisite relief as the Copper Basin. I told her that if I had unfettered power and could have done one thing for one person, it would have been for Emily to find her mother. That this happened is quite possibly the most beautiful thing I have ever witnessed in my entire life.

Sometimes, love and hope wins, even in a place shrouded in darkness and contaminated by poison and violence.

VI.

In the middle of the 1940s, the Copper Basin played host to a desperate battle for political control between the longtime sheriff Burch Biggs and a newly formed group called the Good Government League (GGL). If you are unfamiliar with the way that power is consolidated and acted upon in small rural parts of the Southern Appalachians, the first thing to know is that the sheriff is the be-all, end-all of authority.

In these places, which are too remote and far away from the seats of state and federal power, the county sheriff reigns supreme. In theory, the democratically elected leader of the county – a commissioner in the state of Georgia – should sit at the top of local power structures. However, it is easy to understand why the sheriff's office wields this supremacy instead: they have the guns. Quite literally, it boils down to law enforcement's capacity to compel individuals to bend to their will. They can always lock you up on some trumped-up charge or make your life a living hell by targeting and harassing your family members. Their ability to exercise violent acts grants them influence that outweighs any competing groups – at least, this was the case in the middle of the twentieth century.

But something happened in Polk County, Tennessee in 1946. Veterans had returned from the Second World War and were not the kind of folks that were easily intimidated. Tired of the corruption perpetuated by Biggs and his allies, the veterans organized the GGL and attempted to beat the sheriff at the ballot box.

Biggs, to put it mildly, was not amused by this turn of events. One of my sources told me about bombs being thrown through peoples' windows, about random gunshots striking the outside of homes and cars. It is my understanding that members of both groups engaged in these terroristic and violent tactics. It's a miracle no one died (that we know of).

After the 1946 election, armed men escorted the ballot box from the Ducktown/Copperhill area all the way to the county seat of Benton. A standoff between the competing factions took place in front of the county courthouse, before the National Guard was called in to diffuse the situation. Eventually, Biggs would lose and the GGL would assume leadership.

Their success is still debated to this day. Once in office, the temptation of unbridled power may have proved too much for even the morally righteous members of the GGL. Yet, they were able to defenestrate a leader who acted much like the mafia of New York and New Jersey. By doing so, they helped drag the Copper Basin closer to respectability.

VII.

Surprisingly, the circumstances of Dr. Thomas Hicks' first arrest had to do with his liberal dispensation of opium-based drugs and not human trafficking. Even after Hicks died, these drugs never really left town. When OxyContin, Percocet, and Vicodin were invented in the 1990s, the Copper Basin's aging and impoverished

population became increasingly addicted. Doctors eventually realized the devastation ripping through their community and cut
back on prescribing these medications, but it was too late.

Today, cheap heroin and its exceptionally dangerous cousin
fentanyl are easily brought to the area from the nearby metropolis
of Atlanta, one of the leading drug capitals of the United States of
America.

Some sixty years later, the Copper Basin – like so many other
Appalachian communities – has become roiled by the opioid epidemic. You need only spend a few minutes in one of the Basin's
towns to see these folks. They have that addict look: thin, dishev-
eled, unhappy. More than anything, the addicted are imbued with
a sense of complete and utter hopelessness.

We can't put numbers on these kinds of things, but a significant portion of the area's population is hooked on these drugs. The
future, for them and for their communities, is not bright.

VIII.

There is hope. And it can be found down the road from
Copperhill and McCaysville. If you drive down Georgia Route 5
for about ten miles from the state line, you will come to the town
of Blue Ridge. Geographically and historically, Blue Ridge was
part of the Copper Basin region.

At one time, it was a backwater town called home by only a
few farming families. However, in the late nineteenth century, the
Marietta and North Georgia Railroad established its northern ter-
minus in the town. This had the effect of opening the Copper Basin
to the rapidly growing Atlanta market. Businesses and residential

properties cropped up soon after the establishment of the railroad stop.

A few decades later, Route 76 came to town, opening up the North Georgia Mountains to automobile traffic. The rest, as they say, is history.

Today, if you visited Blue Ridge, you would be hard-pressed to find any remnants of its former identity as an industrial center. Its downtown is filled with expensive shops catering to the Atlanta elite that frequently vacation there. It is easier to find a restaurant with $30 entrees than it is to find a $5 dollar burger. The town has become synonymous with the label "bougie." It is a well-earned moniker.

Despite the gentrification that has transformed downtown Blue Ridge over the last seventy or so years, the rise of the town's economic fortunes has positively affected all the residents who live near it. There are countless jobs offered in the hospitality industry for those people who are the descendants of the original settlers of the region. It is a particularly great place for locals who have an entrepreneurial spirit; indeed, I see new businesses sprouting up in Blue Ridge all the time. I also see new houses being built at a rapid pace. Most of the developers are local in origin and thus employ the area's non-college educated male population.

In the last two or three years, I have watched Blue Ridge's influence creep up Route 5. Wedding venues and housing developments have appeared on the road to Copperhill. The great question for the Copper Basin is this: will Copperhill, Ducktown, and McCaysville go the way of Blue Ridge, or will they continue to backslide into corruption, drug use, and despair?

I know this for sure: I'll be watching, and I'll be rooting for the Copper Basin's success.

The Place of Bricks: Hayden-ville, Ohio

In reality, social space "incorporates" social actions, the actions of subjects both individual and collective who are born and who die, who suffer and who act.

— Henri Lefebvre

I.

It perhaps goes without saying that bricks are some of the world's most mundane objects. Indeed, they are so common that they tend to fade into the background of everyday life, so much so that people rarely – if ever – think about them. However, humans owe much to the invention and perfection of these pedestrian objects. From them we construct our family homes, our public spaces, our places of work, our sidewalks, our streets, and our landscape art. They are why we are not cold in the winter and why our brick-oven pizzas taste so delicious. Ubiquitous and beautiful, bricks are truly the building blocks of modern life.

Of course, someone has to make them – and it's difficult, demanding work. In the Judeo-Christian tradition, perhaps the most famous example comes from Exodus when Moses utters his memorable request, "Let my people go." As a response to this outrageous demand, Pharaoh orders the overseers of the Israelite-slaves "not to supply the people with the straw used in making bricks, as they had done hitherto." And, as a tyrannical leader is wont to do, Pharaoh still demanded that the Israelites produce as many bricks as before, adding with a horrific touch: "Keep these men hard at work; let them attend to that. Take no notice of their lies." In this instance and in many others, the arduous work of brick-making was relegated to slaves or immigrants or what the American poet Walt Whitman would call "bearded roughs." Marginalized peoples, all.

On the other hand, steelmaking has been represented in songs and novels and paintings, with the image of the resolute steelworker and his hardhat burned into our national consciousness. The same is true of coal miners and whalers and cowboys. Yet who has told the story of the lowly brick-maker? What songs sing his praises? What statues of brickmakers adorn public squares? These absences show us that bricks are meant to be seen, but their history is meant to be silent.

But, there is a place in the United States where this enacted silence is easily overcome. Just a short drive over the West Virginia border rests the small village of Haydenville, Ohio. It is a former factory town – or, we should say, a former brick-making factory town.

While the factory and its workers are long gone, their legacy lives on in a very special, very unique way. You see, the brick-workers erected all of the towns' buildings out of the local bricks, and most of these structures are still standing. And they are not made out of ordinary redbricks, either. Haydenville bricks are, quite simply, incredible works of art: they are filled with intricate, swirling lines, and often feature geometric shapes like stars, triangles, and circles. They come in hundreds of varieties and were once sought after by people living all over the United States.

Like mystic hieroglyphics, the bricks of Haydenville, Ohio reveal a secret history of yet another lost American place. What follows is their story.

II.

Given their ubiquity across the globe, it is not all that surprising that bricks are made from two of earth's most common materials: clay and shale. Both are readily available in Haydenville's home region, the Hocking Hills. Throw in enormous supplies of sand, bountiful timber, and even iron and coal deposits, and you get an area perfectly situated for ceramic-related industries. Accordingly, glass, brick, and tile manufactories dominated the regional economy for centuries. Even today, the Anchor Hocking Company makes glassware in nearby Lancaster, Ohio.

Ancient humans used the sun to bake their bricks, but in more recent centuries, the brick industry has employed kilns and other furnaces to create very strong, long-lasting bonds in their finished products. This was the practice of the Haydenville Mining and Manufacturing Company (HMMC), the first major brick factory to be built in the Hocking Hills.

The owner of the company, the eponymous Peter Hayden, engineered an ingenious method to transport the clay mined from the banks of the Hocking River to his factory's furnaces. Knowing that the raw clay was extremely heavy and therefore challenging to move uphill, Hayden constructed a series of tunnels, put rails in them, and had his workers push carts of clay from one end to another. Finished bricks could then be carried on the Hocking Valley Railroad and be distributed to market.

The last factory in Haydenville shut down about sixty years ago and has since been demolished. However, the tunnels remain;

in particular, the one located right outside of Haydenville's Main Street receives attention from ghost hunters, mischievous teenagers, Ohioan historians, and a host of other people. Including me.

It was my youngest sister Jenna who first heard about the Haydenville Tunnel and brought it to my attention. Some years back, several members of my family relocated to the Lancaster, Ohio area. Since I started writing this book, I asked my Ohio family to listen to local stories, to look around, and to tell me about any nearby places that might fit with the general themes of this book. In the fall of 2016, my sister heard about the Tunnel from a friend. So when my wife, daughter, and I came to visit for Thanksgiving, several of us decided to go to Haydenville to try and find the Tunnel and to learn more about the town itself.

On a cold, Northern morning, we began our expedition at the Haydenville Cemetery. As I've mentioned previously, graveyards are the perfect place to start when seeking insight into the past of a lost place. And though I've been to many in the course of researching this project, none affected me as powerfully as this one did.

No one was there but us, a fact that perhaps added to the somber atmosphere and a general sense of gloom. The cemetery itself was in disrepair, though the grass was mowed and it was clear some effort had been put into respecting the dead. There were no grand mausoleums or expensive sandstone headstones; no family plots and no flowers. It was clear that this was the resting place of the poor, of those who toiled in the factory and mines – of those who had died there, too.

Surrounded by the nondescript graves of these dead workers, I found it impossible not to think of Thomas Gray's most famous poem, the one he wrote in a churchyard:

Let not Ambition mock their useful toil,
    Their homely joys, and destiny obscure;
Nor Grandeur hear with a disdainful smile

The short and simple annals of the poor.

The boast of heraldry, the pomp of pow'r,
  And all that beauty, all that wealth e'er gave,
Awaits alike th' inevitable hour.
  The paths of glory lead but to the grave.

Nor you, ye proud, impute to these the fault,
  If Mem'ry o'er their tomb no trophies raise,
Where thro' the long-drawn aisle and fretted vault
  The pealing anthem swells the note of praise.

Like the farmers buried in Gray's rural English churchyard, no trophies mark the burial sites of Haydenville, Ohio's laborers. Instead, many are simply adorned with one or two of the town's most beautiful art-bricks. After all, these (mostly) men had dedicated their entire lives to the production of these objects. They, too, had lived and toiled and died in a factory town in which the company dictated and determined every avenue of life. It is only fitting, then, that their final resting places be designated by the commodities they spent so much time making.

It would be easy to see this cultural practice as a final insult to the dead, as an example of the capitalist system reducing the worker to nothing more than the results of his labor. Like his life, capitalism has robbed him of his death.

And while there is some truth to these sentiments, I see something else in the brick headstones of Haydenville. I see humans doing the best they could, under less than ideal circumstances. These dead men and their families were undoubtedly poor, and couldn't afford, say, the expensive granite headstone of Peter and Alice Hayden. So instead, their buriers selected specific bricks to celebrate the lives of the dead. Perhaps the brick contained a favorite design; or maybe it had an angel on it. Other possibilities beckon.

The act of choosing a gravemarker for someone is an intimate and emotional practice. It is clear to me that the Haydenville brick-headstones were selected with great care and contemplation.

In the intentionality and quiet beauty of the Haydenville graves, I see human warmth and dignity.

III.

Although Haydenville is not very large, it was still somewhat difficult for us to find the Tunnel. After about twenty minutes of searching, we finally stumbled across the entrance. Much to my disappointment, the way in was blocked by several large rectangular pieces of concrete. Scrawled on these monoliths in red graffiti were the names Kate and Bud. A smiley face with Xs for eyes stared at us.

I noticed that a small space in the upper left corner of the tunnel was left open, so I climbed onto a piece of concrete and my wife Jackie passed me a flashlight. I crawled in as far as I could, leaving only my feet dangling on the outside. Flat on my belly, I aimed the flashlight into the Tunnel and took a look into Haydenville's past.

The interior was, predictably, dark and musty and damp. Water dripped from the roof and some light-averse fungi grew from the wet spots on the Tunnel's floor. Strewn all around were elements of the town's former factory life. The functional-turned-ceremonial bricks were there. So, too, were piles of tile that the Haydenville Mining and Manufacturing Company had produced for the construction of urban sanitation networks. There were other materials that my mother's husband Keith – a lifelong resident of this part of Ohio – told me were made when the factory was known as the National Fireproofing Corporation in the 1950s. Graffiti covered the walls. A scent of rot hung in the air.

"It smells like death," I said.

I considered crawling all the way in, but I was concerned I wouldn't be able to climb back out. I am not claustrophobic by any means, nor am I afraid to enter potentially dangerous structures in the name of research and the pursuit of knowledge. However, the fear of my family having to place an embarrassing phone call to the local authorities deterred me from going any further. Slowly I backed out and gave the others a chance to peer into the Tunnel.

While they were doing that, I examined the engineering that made the Tunnel possible. It couldn't have been easy to build; there is quite a lot of what is known as Blackhand Sandstone buried in the surrounding hillside. This extremely strong rock resists erosion, allowing it to stand while its other stone neighbors have long washed away into the Hocking River. This rock is the reason the Hocking Hills even exist; like the sentinel-like basalt towers of the American West, the Blackhand Sandstone formations rise above the glacially-flattened plains of Southeastern, Ohio. They are true testaments to the strength of the Earth and the sublime power of its geologic processes.

Yet, Peter Hayden's workers burrowed their way through it, all in the name of efficiency and profit. They did such a good job that the Tunnel still stands to this day, even as parts of it have caved in. Evidence of their labor has been seared into the scars of the earth, and will likely remain for thousands, if not millions, of years. Like the Roman marble quarries that can be seen from outer space, the Haydenville Tunnel is a symbol of mankind's permanent alteration of the only planet it calls home.

IV.

After exploring the graveyard and the tunnel, we decided to walk into the old factory town. At one time, all the homes in Haydenville were owned by the company and you could only live in one if you were an employee. You were paid in scrip (a form of credit) that could only be redeemed at the Haydenville Mining and Manufacturing Company Store. You went to church with only your fellow workers. And you never left town, which meant you never left the Company.

Slavery, in other words.

Bound by debt and capitalist exploitation, the residents of Haydenville were indeed owned by the Company. Residents of factory towns aren't really human at all; instead, they are beasts of burden who must work from the moment they are born. Like the brick-making Israelites under Pharaoh, they are asked to work harder and harder, to produce more and more, in order to bolster the profits of the Carnegies and Rockefellers and Haydens at the top. What is their compensation for all of this work? Not even decent hourly wages, but instead scorching, paralyzing debt.

But what about Heaven, you might ask, that reward to which the righteous may pass after their earthly toil comes to an end? That too has been proscribed from them, for they are bound by their labor and debt to the Company, aeternum. This denial of heaven to the workers reminds me of the famous twelfth-century icon The Ladder of Divine Ascent, which can be found in Saint Catherine's Monastery in the Sinai Peninsula, one of the world's oldest monasteries.

In the icon, monks ascend a thirty-rung ladder that runs diagonally across the frame. At the top awaits Jesus and the glory

of Heaven, but at the bottom lurks the devil and eternal damna-
tion. Black and winged demons attack the monks with arrows
and ropes, dragging several to the fathomless pit below. Notably,
even the top-most monk, who is the tiniest of distances from his
Savior, is still at risk of being captured by the devil's minions. The
lesson: something is always ready to pull you away from Heaven.
In the case of Haydenville, the black demons are the bosses of the
Haydenville Mining and Manufacturing Company, who ceaseless-
ly drag even their most virtuous and hard-working laborers back
into debasement and suffering.

One particularly insidious way that nineteenth-century companies like the HMMC controlled their workers was through the
manipulation of time. As the renowned humanist geographer Yi-
Fu Tuan has noted, time has a somatic origin: "Time may...be experienced as rhythms of the body: breathing in and out; the alter-
nation of sleep and wakefulness, of energy and fatigue; and as the
rhythmic motions of the body, the arms and legs swinging back
and forth as one walks." Perhaps add to this list the steady beating
of the heart or the rhythmic blinking of the eyes. Tuan goes on to
note that these bodily rhythms are mirrored in the natural world,
including the rising and setting of the sun and seasonal climates.
In my own experience, the origin of time in the human body and
its intimate connection with nature can be most clearly observed
in small children who instinctively wake up when the sun rises and
who fall asleep at dusk.

But what happens when mills need to be run all night? Or
when raw clay must be carted through underground tunnels? Or
when you are paid in credit you must at some later point submit
back to your employer? Or when your rent is deducted from your
wages and you find yourself in a perpetual cycle of debt? Or when
booming factories need constant supplies of labor?

When these factors exist, a person's sense of time is dramatically altered. To put it simply, when someone controls your time, they control you. At the worst extreme, a person whose entire time is controlled by someone else becomes a slave.

The American musician Bruce Springsteen knew this to be true. As a boy, he had watched the men of his hometown Freehold, New Jersey, men like his own father, lose their sense of time and identity after years of hard work in the area's factories and mills. He broaches the subject of labor-induced depersonalization in many of his songs. The workers in Springsteen's music seek refuge and freedom in the dark, when they can race cars and win the hearts of young women, free from the powerful grasp of their employers.

But even the unhappy and listless workers of Springsteen's twentieth-century New Jersey were the benefits of national labor reforms made in the aftermath of brutal strikes and the development of wide scale unionization. They at least had their nights, if not their days. This wasn't necessarily true of men who worked in Haydenville, Ohio and other analogous places in the 1800s.

In nineteenth-century American company towns, it was not unusual to work 16, 17, and even 18 hour days. You couldn't even be guaranteed a full night's sleep. For example, in western railroad towns, schedules would frequently change, so companies would employ young boys to rouse the often drunken and exhausted rail workers. This is dramatized in Willa Cather's novel The Professor's House, when a young Tom Outland must wake up a man named Roddy so he can get to work on time. The time-constrained life of railroad workers is also kept alive by American schoolchildren, who are taught to sing "I've been working on the railroad / All the live long day." Encoded in that second line is the sense that the work day continues as long as a person may live; that is, for the rest of their lives.

Such was the experience of time in Haydenville. It did not belong to the workers. I suspect that any so-called "free time" – and what a loaded and coded phrase that is! – would have been organized and determined by the company. Alienated from nature and from their own bodies, the company town worker existed in a completely totalizing environment.

To repeat: slavery, in other words.

V.

In the early 1970s, most of the homes in Haydenville were added to the National Register of Historic Places (NRHP). What many Americans don't know about the NRHP, however, is that it has no teeth; it has no way to enforce standards of preservation on listed properties. At most, it carries with it a sense of prestige and can serve as a tax break for some property owners.

In Haydenville, the houses are in an increasing state of deterioration. Because of a mediocre local economy, many residents in Hocking County live in relative poverty. The statistics bear this out: Haydenville's current population is far older than Ohio's average, and its residents make significantly less than their fellow Buckeyes. Rampant drug use has hit the area hard, too. Along with nearby West Virginia and Kentucky, Southeastern Ohio is ground zero for the American opioid epidemic. Heroin and fentanyl flood the area from Columbus, one of America's fastest growing cities. One need only take a short glance at the people who walk down the brick sidewalks of Haydenville to see that familiar, zombie-like look of the addicted.

So the people of Haydenville simply don't have the money or the energy to maintain their historic homes. The result is that some are quite literally falling apart, with bricks piled haphazardly in dusty side yards, while some are even overrun with what I call the "aesthetic of abandonment."

Nevertheless, it is easy to envision what Haydenville used to be. No other factory town in the United States, after all, was literally made from the materials made in the factory. And remember, these were beautiful bricks.

From afar, each house looks the same; but when you look at each Haydenville structure up close, you can see that they all feature different brick designs. The achievement is uniformity with a sense of individual expression. And no building quite encapsulates the spirit of Haydenville like its church.

The Haydenville United Methodist Church contains at least twenty different brick designs, all elegantly woven into one another. It also features piping embedded in the façade, leading to a look that some have labeled "sewer pipe gothic." It is gorgeous and its small but active congregation has been able to keep the building in good condition. Amid the surrounding decay, Haydenville's church remains a symbol of the town's past.

It makes sense that the town church would receive special treatment by Peter Hayden and his architects. Christianity was, at least nominally, central to rural American life at this time. And I'm sure Hayden wanted to at least give off the veneer of caring about his workers' souls. I imagine he might have read 1 John 3:18 – which states: "Children, love must not be a matter of theory or talk; it must be true love which shows itself in action" – and felt moved to construct the church.

On the other hand, we might heed the words of Herman Melville's Ishmael, who says "Methinks that in looking at things spiritual, we are too much like oysters observing the sun through the water, and thinking that thick water the thinnest of air." Indeed, one can all too easily see how the Haydenville United Methodist Church served as a commercial display of Peter Hayden's products.

"Look at what we can make! It can be yours! Oh, and we care about our workers too!", it seems to say to me.

Peter Hayden, ever the enterprising capitalist.

VI.

The Haydenville of old, the self-styled "last Ohio company town," is no more. Like the other places I've examined in this book, it is lost and what remains of it physically-speaking is increasingly ruinous. There is no more Haydenville Mining and Manufacturing Company, no more company store, no more rail-carts running through the tunnel, no more artisanal bricks coming out of the furnace; no more town-wide church services; all of this is lost. A globalized and permanently changed American economy put an end to all of it.

In his 1995 song, "Youngstown," Bruce Springsteen narrates the decline of another Ohio place. Although Youngstown is two hundred miles away from Haydenville and was once centered on steelmaking, the two places are connected by the feeling of abandonment and despair that follows in the wake of extreme economic change. In this song, a narrator speaks to an amorphous entity called simply, you.

Who is this you? On one hand, it's easy to cast it as the capitalist owners of factories. Is Bruce singing about Peter Hayden? Because it sounds an awful lot like he is. However, there's another way of interpreting that pronoun, one that hits far closer to home. We are the "you." It's us. Because haven't we all benefitted from the industrial production of places like Youngstown and Haydenville? The walkways, roads, and sanitation systems of many of the United States' major cities were made with Haydenville brick and tile. Places like Haydenville and Youngstown literally built the United States. So it's worth pointing out that all of us, all Americans, were enriched by these places and the men who toiled in them. But we – like the Peter Haydens of the world – have forgotten them. In Haydenville, these men were once slaves to the company, living a harsh and unforgiving existence. Then, once the money wasn't there to be made anymore, they were abandoned and subsequently forgotten. This whole story is a tragedy and we are all complicit in it.

Today, if the economic and social fortunes of Hocking and its surrounding counties don't improve, soon too the factory town's historic buildings will be reduced to rubble. Indeed, the current residents of Haydenville have few, if any, ties to the industry that once dominated every facet of life in the town. It doesn't mean anything to them. Why should they care about preserving its memory? In another fifty years, I ask, will there be anything left?

In my time in Haydenville, I've felt a sense that many of the people who live there have closed themselves off from the world – and, perhaps, even from each other (and maybe for good reason). One hundred years ago, everyone in Haydenville would have known one another; it would have been a literal face-to-face community. But now? Somehow I doubt that the residents of Haydenville even know who lives at the end of their street. Without the totalizing power of the Company to bind them together, today's residents of Haydenville are adrift.

Like the places I've explored in the previous chapters, there is no going back. A different future awaits, but I find it hard to be anything but pessimistic and grim about what that future will entail.

VII.

Haydenville's legacy, however, will survive as long as the bricks it once made do. And those bricks were exceptionally well made. Allow me to explain. In the almost two years since I've been researching Haydenville for this project, I've come across its bricks in a number of places, some quite unexpected.

I have found them in the town of Roanoke, Virginia, when on one road trip, my family and I stopped off of Interstate 81 for lunch. While looking for a place to eat, we noticed we were walking on a sidewalk made out of Haydenville bricks. In the town of Sugar Grove, Ohio, where my mother and sister now live, a house near the edge of the village is made out of them. In Columbus, where Peter Hayden and his wife are interred, countless structures feature the bricks that were once made two hours to the south. And during one fall break spent in Savannah, Georgia, I discovered that Haydenville's art-bricks line the walkways of the city's stunning Colonial Park Cemetery. What a strange yet lovely combination exists in that graveyard: there's the eerie above-ground graves, the gently flowing Spanish moss in the trees, and the beautiful bricks from Haydenville, Ohio.

To some extent, this brick diaspora isn't all that surprising; after all, the Haydenville Mining and Manufacturing Company made a lot of bricks. They also brought them to the 1904 World's Fair in Saint Louis, Missouri – even winning an award for best "outside brick in floor." In a showcase for the world, Peter Hayden advertised his special bricks to overseas buyers, and I am told that they can be found in many of the European capital cities.

I'm sure I'll keep looking for them for the rest of my life. And after reading this I hope you will, too.

No More Wilderness:
The Lost Communities
of the North Shore

In an older part of the cemetery he saw some people strolling. Elderly gent with a cane, his wife on his arm. They did not see him. They went on among the titled stones and rough grass, the wind coming from the woods cold in the sunlight. A stone angel in her weathered marble robes, the downcast eyes. The old people's voices drift across the lonely space, murmurous above these places of the dead. The lichens on the crumbling stones like a strange green light. The voices fade. Beyond the gentle clash of weeds. He sees them stoop to read some quaint inscription and he pauses by an old vault that a tree has half dismantled with its growing. Inside there is nothing. No bones, no dust. How surely are the dead beyond death. Death is what the living carry with them. A state of dread, like some uncanny foretaste of a bitter memory. But the dead do not remember and nothingness is not a curse. Far from it.
— Cormac McCarthy, Suttree

He had taken a dreary road, darkened by all the gloomiest trees of the forest, which barely stood aside to let the narrow path creep through, and closed immediately behind. It was all as lonely as could be; and there is this peculiarity in such a solitude, that the traveller knows not who may be concealed by the innumerable

trunks and the thick boughs overhead; so that with lonely foot-
steps he may yet be passing through an unseen multitude.
     — Nathaniel Hawthorne, "Young Goodman Brown"

I.

On a hot and thundery summer day, I paddled a kayak across
the enormous expanse of western North Carolina's Lake Fontana.
The result of a World War II era damming project, Fontana is lo-
cated in one of the most remote areas of the Eastern United States.
It is bracketed by the massive peaks of the Great Smoky Mountains
National Park to the north and the likewise gigantic Snowbird and
Yellow Creek Mountains to the south. A single road, NC-68, runs
along its southern shore.

This is not a party lake, like Kentucky's Lake Cumberland or
Georgia's Lake Lanier. On Fontana there are few houseboats or
speedboats or canoes or jet skis, no marina lounges or floating tiki
bars. It is a quiet place. Here, you usually see more ospreys than
people.

It was thus not the least bit surprising to me that I was all alone
on this particular August day.

I was headed to what is left of Proctor, a community that was
displaced because of the construction of Fontana Dam. Every
few minutes, thundercracks boomed overhead. I kept thinking,
over and over, that I shouldn't be out on the water. The Smoky
Mountains are deceiving, though – one can hear thunder from
far, far away. I have spent days in those mountains when I've heard
echoing booms for hours but never saw a single drop of rain.
Nevertheless, the nearby thunder made my trip across the lake an
especially tense one.

As I paddled, I kept thinking to myself that this was what Ralph Waldo Emerson meant by self-reliance. It was up to me – and me only – to arrive safely. If I had a problem, I alone must solve it. I had to navigate successfully and have the physical fitness and endurance necessary to complete such a journey. If I failed in some way, I could literally die. These were heavy thoughts to ponder.

With aching arms I finally approached the mouth of Hazel Creek, a gorgeous stream that begins its long descent to Fontana Lake from the highest reaches of the second tallest mountain in the East, the monstrous Clingman's Dome. The sight of Hazel provided a sense of relief; it meant that I had found the right place. I still faced a significant hike to Proctor and its two nearby grave-yards, but at least I had made it across the lake in one piece.

As I tied my kayak to a tree and changed into dry clothes, I meditated on the difficulty of the journey. I kept thinking: this is what it takes to get here, a seven mile round trip boat ride. Either that or a 15 mile hike from the big dam. There's no way around it: getting to Proctor is fucking hard.

I remember thinking, "if this trip is this hard on me – a healthy man in his early 30s – it must be nearly impossible for the relatives of those buried in Proctor's cemeteries." They are inching closer to the grave now themselves, these grayheaded octogenarians with their walkers and canes and thick Appalachian accents. To visit their dead and commune with their ancestors, they face miles of open water and tortuous unmotorized mountain trails.

It should go without saying, but taking care of the dead is a cultural phenomenon that is at the very heart of the human experience. It is so basic to us, that every single human culture around the world practices it. Our complex systems of mourning and memory separate us from the other animals – these are quintessentially human activities, full of deep symbolism and meaning. To prevent people from performing their own cultural tradition of remembrance because of a government-mandated construction project is nothing short of a violation of their sovereign human rights. This is the kind of despotic stunt that nation-states like North Korea regularly stage. And yet, right here in the United States of America – within one of our supposed greatest achievements, a national park – lies a textbook definition of state-based tyranny.

As unbelievable as this may sound, it is the true reality of those who were displaced from Proctor.

These people were once promised a road that would connect their former hometowns to civilization, but the federal government never completed the project. The small section of road that was built is now itself deteriorating, and has earned the appropriate moniker of "The Road to Nowhere." Like the people of the Minisink, the treatment of the residents of the North Shore is a shining example of what the government of the United States can and will do to its own people.

But theirs isn't the first displacement from this place; in fact, there have been several waves of human habitation on the North Shore of the Little Tennessee River. There have been Paleo peoples, the Mississippians, the Cherokee, the CCC, the loggers, the sportsmen, and the outlaws. Viewed collectively, what emerges is a story about a place that has been fought over since the first humans found it some 15,000 years ago. Despite the presence of the national park, I see very little that suggests this battle will end any time soon.

II.

Most people don't know it, but not all of the Cherokee Indians were forced onto the Trail of Tears. Instead, a small group led by the rebel Tsali fought against Andrew Jackson's policy of removal. Their hideout and home base? The North Shore.

The Cherokee had probably come to this part of the Blue Ridge Mountains after it had been vacated by the Mississippian peoples. This would have been sometime in the vicinity of 1600 or so. They found empty villages and empty earthen mounds that used to be the center of those places. The Cherokee then set up shop and began to flourish.

However, the discovery of gold in some of the area rivers led to disputes with the whites over ownership of the land. Several skirmishes were fought between the two sides. Eventually, the whites won. And they wanted not just some of the land – they wanted it all.

As the legend goes, one morning Tsali and his family were disturbed by gun-toting whites and were ordered to leave their homeland. The details are murky and definitely fall in the realm of hearsay, but it's believed that one of Tsali's children was killed in cold blood. He met this violence with violence of his own. After all, this was a guy who had fought in the Creek Wars. He was a warrior through and through. You don't just walk all over a person like him and expect it to go well.

Tsali succeeded in killing his captors. He then fled to the Smokies, taking refuge in the very tall and imposing mountains of the North Shore. He was joined by several hundred Cherokee refugees who refused to step foot on the Trail of Tears. They survived by using their local knowledge of the terrain in much the same way as the New England tribes did during conflicts like King Philip's War and the French and Indian War. They found enough food through hunting and the gathering of wild plants.

Although Tsali didn't know it, negotiations were taking place between Cherokee elders and the leaders of the military unit dispatched by Jackson. The whites ultimately offered Tsali and his group a deal. If he was willing to surrender, they would allow the refugees under his protection to stay in the Blue Ridge Mountains.

I often wonder why he decided to take the deal. What reason did he have to trust these people? It seems highly unlikely to me that he would have done so without some serious reassurance as to the validity of this proposal. We will never know, however.

Tsali did take the deal. He surrendered and the whites murdered him, his brother, and some of his sons. To make matters even worse, members of Tsali's own tribe were forced to kill him in a firing squad. As with many of the stories relating to the native peoples found in this book, what becomes crystal clear is the barbarity and cruelty of the white Americans.

Nevertheless, Tsali was successful. The several hundred refugees were allowed to stay. Thanks to his sacrifice, their descendants still live in the area today. If you ever travel to Cherokee, North Carolina you could meet some of them.

III.

The first white settlers came to the valleys around Hazel Creek in the first few decades of the 1800s. They would have about a century's worth of time there before their land would be taken away from them by their own government.

During this century, these settlers of the backcountry lived off the bounty of the land, as the Mississippians had done before them, and as their neighbors the Cherokee continued to do. For example, the Little Tennessee River has over 30 species of fish, as well as several types of shellfish, all of which are edible. The river is and has been a literal life-giver to those who live along its banks. The surrounding forest also offered berries that could be harvested and canned for the winter months, several types of nuts, and plenty of mushrooms. Deer, bear, and small game were abundant and provided families with meat that they would preserve through smoking and curing. When it came to the essentials necessary for human survival, the North Shore region was quite a good place to call home.

These settlers were also connected to other communities on the Tennessee side of the Smoky Mountains like Cades Cove, as well as to the towns of Bryson City and Robbinsville in North Carolina. Knoxville was further away, but achievable through navigation of rudimentary roads, which often ran on top of old Native American trade routes. Networks of kin were thus spread across the mountains and the residents of the area frequently moved back and forth over them.

The mountain people also developed a distinctive culture that still exists in the Blue Ridge and Smokies. They fashioned home-made instruments and created a quintessentially American sound that ultimately gave rise to the genres of country, bluegrass, and gospel. They worshipped the Christian God in plain yet beautiful wooden churches. They told stories of the Boojum and forged relationships with the Eastern Band of the Cherokee Indians that persist to this day. In many ways, these people were living classic American lives: they were unburdened by government, free, and content.

But, as the nineteenth century gave way to the twentieth, something was notably lacking in Proctor and the other Hazel Creek communities: electricity. With the Industrial Revolution of the previous century providing unprecedented material and financial development, the federal government of the United States began looking for ways to provide power to the more remote reaches of the country. Early hydroelectric dams were thus constructed downstream of Proctor on the Little Tennessee in the first twenty years or so of the 1900s. The government and the Knoxville-based

Alcoa Corporation began looking at a potential dam site fairly close to Proctor during the 1930s, but disagreements about cost and labor prevented anything from being built.

And then the Japanese bombed Pearl Harbor in 1941 and everything changed. Within a month, the Fontana Dam project was underway. The writing was on the wall for the North Shore communities: they would have to move or watch their homes be flooded.

IV.

Right before you cross the boundary into the Great Smoky Mountains National Park on Lakeshore Drive, you pass a po-em-sign that reads:

WELCOME TO
THE ROAD TO NO-WHERE
A BROKEN PROMISE!
1943 - ?
NO MORE WILDERNESS

As the environmentalist Bill McKibben has argued, wilderness occupies a privileged (and arguably religious) role in American public life. It is something that cannot be questioned. It is assumed that wilderness is inherently good and should be protected at all costs. If you say you are against wilderness, you risk becoming a social pariah. Who could oppose such a glorious concept?

Well, people who have been mistreated, neglected, and demonized in the name of wilderness, that's who. As I mentioned at the beginning of this chapter, the Appalachians who were displaced from Proctor and the other North Shore communities were once promised a road that would enable them to visit their ancestors' graves. But because of "environmental concerns" that road was never completed. Only a few miles of it were ever constructed. They make their anger and their heartbreak quite obvious in the above-mentioned sign.

So, to see all of this for myself, I ventured down the Road to Nowhere on an early December day during an unseasonably warm spell. I passed no cars on my way in. When I got to the end of the road, there was no one parked there. This is, indeed, one of the most remote parts of the Eastern U.S. No one comes down the Road to Nowhere, especially on a weekday during the National Park's off-season.

Near the end of the drivable section of the road is a large tunnel that was built at significant cost, but never used as intended. Like the tunnel in Haydenville, Ohio, this abandoned one is filled with graffiti and a pervasive sense of injustice. As I ventured through it on foot, I couldn't help but think of its emptiness as a reflection of the emptiness of the promise once made to the Appalachians.

When one is aware of the nasty history that lurks behind the veneer of this most visited of the National Parks – one of our country's ostensible "crown jewels" – it is hard to perceive the landscape in any other way. For me, the National Park is beautiful, yes. But it is also a place brimming with what the African-American writer Toni Morrison calls "rememory."

Consider these lines, which are spoken by the ex-slave Sethe in Morrison's seminal work Beloved:

I was talking about time. It's so hard for me to believe in it. Some things go. Pass on. Some things just stay. I used to think it was my rememory. You know. Some things you forget. Other things you never do. But it's not. Places, places are still there. If a house burns down, it's gone, but the place – the picture of it – stays, and not just in my rememory, but out there, in the world....Someday you be walking down the road and you hear something or see something going on. So clear. And you think it's you thinking it up. A thought picture. But no. It's when you bump into a rememory that belongs to someone else.

As I walked along the liminal section of paved road that is on the other side of the Road to Nowhere's tunnel, I found myself bumping into other people's rememories. I could see the Appalachians removing plank after plank from their former homes (they didn't want to waste the wood, of course), piling them onto a horse-drawn wagon, and pulling away from the place they had made for themselves. I could see the tears of their children, who were witnessing the literal demolition of their childhood. I could see the last goodbyes made between neighbors and between the living and the dead. I could hear the promises to return, the utterances of memory and devotion. I could see congregations worshipping one last time together in the piney woods, offering up prayers that undoubtedly went unanswered. I could see – and feel – all of this, their suffering, their pain, their displacement, and their fury.

I decided then and there that I would walk as far into the backcountry as I could reasonably handle in one day. To look and to feel. To see what ghosts still roamed the North Shore.

V.

Once home to many small villages, the North Shore is now one of the largest unroaded wildernesses in the American East. Although Great Smoky Mountains is the most visited of all the National Parks, most tourists don't leave the safety of the main roads and well-traveled areas. This is for the best, since many people have died in this Park when they've ventured off of trails or gotten otherwise lost. So despite all of the people that regularly flood the Park, it is quite easy to elude them.

On the day I walked deep into the backcountry of the North Shore, I did not see another human for almost 12 hours. I was literally the only person around for miles and miles and miles. I have never in my life felt such utter and complete isolation.

I decided to head to Forney Creek, a trout stream of some renown, and to hike along it for some miles before reconnecting with the main trail and the Road to Nowhere.

One of the things you notice in such remote country is the lack of human sound. Even if you live in a rural place like I do, you are always surrounded by the sounds of people. You hear cars on the road, the hum of your house's machines, airplanes roaring overhead. But in the North Shore, you hear none of this.

What becomes most apparent to the ears is the sound of the wind. Even on quiet days, the air still rushes down off of Clingman's Dome, pervading the entire region. It is a beautiful yet lonely sound, one that you only notice when immersed in such empty terrain. For me, the sound of this wind is the sound of nothingness, and is the thing that most cemented the reality of the North Shore's forced abandonment. Once those woods were filled with the sounds of sawblades, the crack of gunshots, and the singing of churchgoers; now, only the sound of the mountain remains.

But no matter how much time moves forward, the rememories of the Appalachians stay rooted in the landscape. If you look closely, you can find physical signs of their lives.

Several miles deep into the woods, I came across a solitary chimney that remains standing in the open air, even as the entirety of the rest of the house has decayed into the surrounding loam. A silent sentinel, if you will, to a way of live destroyed. Nearby, I uncovered a former trash heap, which was replete with broken pieces of pottery and other discarded items.

Deeper yet, I came across several iron bars situated on the edge of Forney Creek. These were remnants from the logging operations that provided steady income to the North Shore communities. Where an environmentalist sees the epitome of evil, I see a way of life that was central to the success of many mountain communities. And though the primeval forests that they felled can never be recovered, they have been replaced with new old growth. These woods haven't been logged in almost a century, now, and are well on their way to recovery. I'd much rather be one of these trees than the poor people who were thrown off their land.

Eventually, I made my way back to my car. As I drove down the Road to Nowhere, I spotted a small cemetery plot located on the lakeside of the road. It had no path to it, nor had it been given much care. Yet, in it rests someone's ancestor. In sunken and forgotten graves, the dead still inhabit the North Shore.

VI.

As if their displacement from their homes wasn't enough of an insult, many of the North Shore's residents were "given the opportunity" to construct the dam that was at the center of all this trauma. Imagine having to make this decision. I doubt very many of the Appalachians wanted to build the dam that would cause them to lose their homes. However, jobs in the mountains weren't easy to come by and the government was offering gainful employment, so many displaced peoples ended up making this decision.

The United States set up a temporary community in a holler called Welch Cove. Thousands of people ended up there and the settlement was given the name Fontana. It was a prosperous little city in the middle of nowhere, replete with a grocery store, a theatre, baseball fields, and multiple churches of different Protestant denominations. Building an almost 500 foot dam on a very large river takes a lot of people, a lot of labor, and a lot of concrete. All of this came together in Fontana.

After the dam was constructed and the Little Tennessee River was finally impounded, many of the Appalachians left for Robbinsville or Bryson City or even Marysville and Knoxville. The former construction town was then converted into a resort which is still in operation.

On a hot and humid summer day, I drove my family to the Fontana Village Resort and Marina. It is an odd place. On one hand, there's a lazy river and a very nice pool filled with vacationing tourists, most of whom come from the cities of central Tennessee. There's an ice cream shop, a few restaurants, a mini-golf course, and many little bungalows and cabins.

On the other hand, the history of the place is abundantly clear. The general store that serves the tourists was once the construction community's company store. The cabins that people stay in for the week once housed the displaced families from towns like Proctor. The baseball field is the same one that little Appalachian children played on while their fathers built Fontana Dam. And finally, an original nineteenth-century cabin has been relocated and placed right in the middle of the resort, highlighting the former history of the area.

I spoke with some employees, most of whom either lived at the resort during its busy season or commuted from Robbinsville, and very few of them knew much about the history of the location. This is not at all surprising. Concepts of deep history and rememory are not important to those folks who are simply trying to earn a paycheck and get by. Nevertheless, there's a very high probability that the families of those I spoke with were affected by the construction of the dam and the formation of the national park. Yet the forces that have pulled at their lives remain unnoticed by them.

And if the workers of Fontana Village have only a vague understanding of the traumatic events that enabled that place to emerge out of the Western North Carolinian wilderness, the tourists know next to nothing. They're just there for a good time. It's hard to blame them, either.

Once the scene of one of the largest forced relocations in history of the Appalachian Mountains, Fontana Village's afterlife is one of leisure and fun for visitors and an important source of employment for area residents. There are worse outcomes than this.

VII.

This story doesn't end where you expect it to. Yes, there's a beautiful national park and a lovely cold water lake. Yes, there's now electricity running through even the most remote parts of the Southern Appalachians. Yes, the wound of the North Shore's displacement is still fresh and will never quite heal. But something even more horrifying came out of this whole situation, something that was kept extremely quiet by the American government during the dam's construction.

The story of the North Shore ends with the dropping of two nuclear warheads on Hiroshima and Nagasaki. Unbeknownst even to the Tennessee Valley Authority, the United States had set up another temporary city on the other side of the Smoky Mountains. Oak Ridge, as it became known, was the location of the Manhattan Project. Fontana Dam provided power to the Alcoa Company so that it could rapidly construct an aluminum-based Air Force. This freed up the dam on the Clinch River to provide all of its power to Oak Ridge.

Building a nuclear bomb takes massive amounts of energy. According to the official TVA history of its role in the development of the atomic bomb, hydroelectric power helped the Oak Ridge engineers to build "the centrifuge and the electromagnetic and gaseous-diffusion processes." Eventually, enough power was drawn out of the mountains to complete the Fat Man and Little Boy bombs that were dropped on the Japanese mainland, accelerating their defeat and bringing about the end of World War II.

There is a direct line that can be drawn between the displacement of the North Shore communities, their resettlement in Fontana Village, the construction of Fontana Dam, and the deaths of hundreds of thousands of Japanese. And it is a sad, sad line to draw.

Considered by some to be one of the great human rights violations in the history of humanity, many historians and cultural critics forget about the suffering that happened on the American end of this momentous historical occurrence. And while I don't believe that displacement and coerced labor rise to the same level as wide-scale nuclear destruction, it should at least be noted that the Manhattan Project created significant trauma and pain within the United States itself.

Such singular events rarely leave anyone unscathed.

VIII.

And yet, what are we left with? There's a 480 foot concrete monstrosity that still holds back the Little Tennessee. There's a Road to Nowhere. There's enormous expanses of wilderness. There's trauma and ghosts and rememories galore. Yet most people who visit the

Great Smoky Mountains National Park or even Fontana Dam itself have no idea what transpired there, and what immense human suffering these creations have wrought.

Such is the point of this chapter. I believe it is still possible to enjoy the National Park and to marvel at the incredible engineering that made the dam, all while still recognizing the human toll that made both of these things possible. What I wish for is contemplation, meditation, and an embrace of the rememories that pervade this most unique of places. Doing this helps in several ways.

Firstly, it facilitates a deeper and more nuanced understanding of what government intervention can do to human life. For example, things like national parks do not emerge out of vacuums. There are always people who are hurt by the creation of public lands, and these people are almost always the poor and the marginalized. It's far easier to kick the destitute out than it is to displace the rich. This has always been the case and it will remain a quintessential part of the American story. Show me I'm wrong; I'd like to see you try.

Furthermore, interventions of this sort do things to the natural world that are difficult, if not impossible, to reverse. I mourn for the loss of the Little Tennessee River's ecosystem. Even if Fontana Dam were somehow miraculously decommissioned and removed, there's no easy way to replicate what that watershed was like previously. It's gone forever.

And finally, being aware of the traumatic history embedded in the North Shore can help remind us that ultimately it is up to the American people to decide the fate of this land. Let me be absolutely clear: just because much of it is protected by national park status doesn't mean that it will always be so. For example, the Trump administration aggressively rolled back protections for other designated public lands, such as the Bears Ears and Grand Staircase-Escalante National Monuments. Do you really think that just because a piece of American soil is called a "national park" instead of a "national monument" that it is forever protected from destruction? The history of the North Shore, with all of its various displacements, demands that we not overlook the possibility that someday this territory will be taken away from us, the citizens of the United States.

For these and many other reasons, I hope that the history of the North Shore remains a part of the public consciousness. A worrisome future, indeed, awaits those who intentionally efface the suffering of the past.

Heart-Shaped Hot Tubs and Honeymoons: The Lost Resorts of the Pocono Mountains

Will you seek afar off? you surely come back at last,
In things best known to you finding the best, or as good as the best,
In folks nearest to you finding the sweetest, strongest, lovingest,
Happiness, knowledge, not in another place but this place, not for another hour but this hour
— Walt Whitman, "A Song for Occupations"

I.

On a cold Sunday night in late November, the main hall of the Mountain Manor Inn caught fire. Dramatic drone video showed that the flames leapt over a hundred feet into the black Pocono night; the fire was so intense that the emergency workers simply let it burn. After all, the building had been abandoned for over six years. The only guests staying at Mountain Manor on that evening in 2018 were rodents and weeds. There was nothing to protect.

In a sign of the lightning-fast communications of our times, my fellow Pocono expatriate Lauren sent me a text message: "Do you know Mountain Manor is burning?" In response, I immediately texted our friend Mike, who still lives there, and declared in all capitals: "MOUNTAIN MANOR IS ON FUCKING FIRE!!" This was not news to him. He had been blocked from driving home on Creek Road because of the inferno. He said you could see the fire for miles lit up in the red-black sky. Every fire truck in the area was on scene. It was chaos.

After a moment of thought, I shot Lauren a text: "Well, there goes a part of our childhood."

II.

We had all worked there. For Lauren, it was her first job: a waitress in the very building that burned down. Same for my sister Kristin, who bussed tables alongside Lauren. For me, it may have been my third or fourth job. I was an attendant at the amusement park across the street, delightfully named Thunder Creek Quarry. I worked there along with our other friends Will and Danielle; it was our jobs to make sure little New Yorkers didn't kill themselves while driving go-karts or bumper boats. It was hot. There were a lot of bees. But I loved every minute of it.

Beyond our early forays into the world of employment, Mountain Manor served as a backdrop to our rural, mountainous childhood. The road that slices through the property is one of the only ways up to the mountain where we all lived. To go to the grocery store, we drove by Mountain Manor. On the way to school, we drove by Mountain Manor. To get to New Jersey or New York or anywhere really, we drove by Mountain Manor.

It once had six golf courses – six! It had a tennis court, a pool, even an ice skating rink. It had a basketball court where Kristin once got hit in the head by a ball, giving her the indignity of her very first concussion. It had an arcade, a bingo room, and mini-golf.

It had hundreds of rooms scattered over countless acres. I remember seeing them, the tourists, decked out in their golfing clothes: polo shirts and khakis; sweaters tied behind necks. I remember the Jaguars and Mercedeses and Lexuses that they drove, cars that spoke of a life so different than ours.

Even when I worked there, there were rumors that the owners, the Scott family, were looking to sell the property. We all believed that Larry Simon, the local land baron, would scoop it up and slap together his shittily-made homes to sell to unsuspecting and ignorant New Yorkers. There were rumors that someone from Japan would buy it.

None of this happened, though parts of it did eventually get sold – some of the former hotel rooms were converted into rental properties. However, most of it, including the six golf courses and the main building that burned, fell into disrepair. On trips back to my former home region, I'd chart the progress of the regrowing forest, which greedily sought to reclaim the golf courses. The wild brown trout in Marshalls Creek flourished once the property was no longer poisoned by the chemicals that are necessary to keep such manicured and controlled spaces looking perfect. During these years, Mountain Manor's deterioration taught me a valuable lesson: nature is the most patient of entities, always ready to take back what once belonged to it.

And Mountain Manor wasn't and isn't alone. So many properties – Birchwood, Fernwood, Penn Hills, Alpine Mountain, the list goes on and on and on – all stand in a state of abandonment. They are gone; they are lost.

As some of my readers probably remember, the Poconos was once one of America's leading honeymoon destinations. Come consummate your new love in a heart-shaped bed or in a champagne-glass hot tub, the ads would say! The Poconos weren't just beautiful like the Adirondacks or the Catskills or the Blue Ridge

Mountains – they were romantic, damn it! Long before Virginia was for Lovers, the Poconos was the sexiest place on earth.

But now, all of this love, all of this romance and lust and sex, all of it is just ash and dust.

III.

In 1867, one year after his family expanded their resort to accommodate two hundred guests, L. W. Brodhead published The Delaware Water Gap: Its Scenery, Its Legends and Early History. Descended from one of the first white settlers of the mountainous region later called the Poconos, Brodhead was a shrewd businessman and an aspiring sentimentalist author. He recognized that he could attract more guests to his Kittatinny House by circulating a text that contained a series of invented myths, exaggerated (at best) histories, and juicy tales regarding the Lenape or "Minsi" Indians. Published in Philadelphia by Caxton Press, his book had the intended effect, generating strong sales and encouraging stage-coach and railroad traffic to his majestic hotel on the Delaware River. After all, who wouldn't want to see the waterfall where the Indian "Princess" Winona leapt to her death after learning that her white lover couldn't marry her and had to return to New York City?

Brodhead's sensational book was so popular that a second edition was published in 1870, in which he attempted to fend off criticism of his project, declaring: "It will be difficult for those who read what is here given, to divest their minds of the opinion that it is written in the interest of the Kittatinny House. The relation the writer sustains to the place would make the inference natural, hence much delicacy is felt in placing it before the public; but he hopes for a more liberal appreciation of his motives on the part of the intelligent class of readers who visit the Water Gap." Make no mistake: the book was written "in the interest of the Kittatinny House." And it worked fabulously.

In part because of Brodhead's book and in part because of the stunning beauty of the mountains, people couldn't get enough of the Poconos in the postbellum United States. For example, the major newspapers of the day in all of the large East Coast cities ran columns describing the beauty of the area and published lists of railroad departures, navigable roads, and other logistical information meant to help city dwellers plan their trips to the mountains. Residents of the area responded by erecting luxurious, all-inclusive resorts that catered to the urban wealthy, as well as lodging houses for the rustic-minded sportsmen who sought the area's native brook trout and white-tailed deer. Tourism was always the area's leading industry and was specifically responsible for the growth of the towns and small cities that still comprise the region today.

When Interstate 80 was opened through the Delaware Water Gap in 1953, the number of tourist visitors to the Poconos – which was already high – exploded. Pocono families continued to meet that demand by opening new resorts and hotels, and by the end of the decade hundreds of places of hospitality were open for business. By this time, the Poconos had become the go-to location for America's honeymooners.

What began with Brodhead's romanticization of the Pocono landscape ended with the aforementioned heart-shaped beds and hot tubs and champagne-glass Jacuzzis. In the place where Winona's love for her Dutch boyfriend Hendrick was denied consummation, the marriages of countless others were.

And for a while, traveling lovers and young families sustained the region's economy. But by the time the new millennium hit, changes in the structure of the American and mid-Atlantic economies were headed the Poconos' way. Airfare had cheapened dramatically, making it much easier for residents of New York and

Philadelphia to fly to, say, the Caribbean. Even the beautiful water-falls and cool forests of the Poconos are no match for the sand and surf of Jamaica. Large companies began purchasing the remaining resorts and what was once a family-run industry became deeply corporatized. In the middle of the twentieth-century, most of the profits from the tourism industry stayed in the Poconos; by the year 2000, much of it was sent out of the area and into the pockets of the very wealthy.

Then, the financial crisis of 2008 happened. Monroe and Pike Counties were at the epicenter of the subprime loan debacle and the region's entire economy teetered on the verge of collapse. This was the death-knell for many Pocono resorts. The dwindling families who still vacationed in the Poconos suddenly couldn't afford to do so anymore. The owners of the hotels and resorts went bankrupt, and because of the conditions of the national and global economy, they were unable to find buyers for their large, deteriorating prop-erties. They were thus abandoned.

In the decade since the Great Recession, most of these aban-doned resorts have fallen into an increasing state of disrepair, and the area economy has yet to fully heal. L.W. Brodhead's dream of a prosperous Pocono region driven by tourism had finally died. Nothing has yet taken its place. Perhaps nothing ever will.

IV.

The original Quaker tourists from Philadelphia came for the peaceful repose offered by the remote and rugged woods. They used this isolation for meditation and prayer. The anglers that followed, too, were drawn to the region by its natural offerings: in this case, the abundance of its wildlife and its out-of-the-way, backcountry atmosphere. Even the honeymooners of the twentieth century came to find romance amid the beauty of Pocono nature. This is my home region's most striking characteristic and the one most vitally important to its past, present, and future.

As children, my friends and sisters and I had intimate access to this nature. It was always already there, just waiting right outside our doors. We played in it and on it and through it, for countless hours on countless days. We ate it and drank it. We used it to build our homes and grow our gardens. We fought it and lost – scratches, tick bites, burns, car accidents, concussions, broken bones. We fought it and won – brook trout sliced down their bellies, with their pink meat shining in the sun; felled white-tailed deer filling winter freezers; trees chainsawed, dried, stacked, and burned in stoves.

Even today, this nature is never far from my mind. It catches me at the oddest moments: stuck in traffic, an eyeblink in the classroom, a stray memory during a meeting. It is the dominant feature of my dreamscapes. It is where I go in my mind; in many ways, it is my mind...and body, too. I cannot dissever my identity from it. I never could. It is me and I am it.

Allow me to describe it to you.

Giant boulders, deposited during the last period of glaciation, cast grand shadows over the mossy forest floor. As children we dreamed that a race of long-dead giants had placed them there. Little did we realize that indeed a giant was responsible, one miles thick with ice, so powerful it could reshape the very earth itself.

When the giant retreated as the planet warmed some 12,000 years ago, it dug its claws deep into the ground and scratched and scraped and dragged and pulled. In a goodbye embrace, the giant scarred the Pocono landscape forever.

The result was a land stripped bare, exposed and naked, strewn with huge sandstone monoliths. Into the depressions dug out by the glacier-giant came water from the sky, forming lakes, swamps, and vernal ponds. You cannot walk a quarter mile in any direction in any Pocono forest and not come to a swamp. It is as much a swampland as it is a forestland.

The swamps and lakes form creeks that drain toward the east, toward the Delaware River and New Jersey. Before they reach that big river and the land beyond, the creeks plunge over the edge of the mountains. This results in hundreds of beautiful waterfalls, including the one where Princess Winona is said to have died for her forbidden love.

In the winter, we skated across the frozen surfaces of the swamps, leaping from one grass clump to another. If we were unlucky, the ice would break and our feet would be plunged into the foul-smelling detritus below. In summer we gathered by the thousands the huckleberries that grow everywhere in those wetlands. In the boreal bogs, we looked suspiciously upon the pitcher plants and sundews, wondering how plants could eat animals and what this meant and whether they were interested in eating us.

On the rocky forest floor, wildflowers form a regal carpet. Their names, learned from the old and from books and from each other, called out: here's a starflower! here's a lady's slipper! here's miterwort and foamflower and marsh marigold and skunk cabbage!

In the canopy above, birds up for the summer from the jungle-mountains of South America and the Caribbean display a veritable smorgasbord of color: Peruvian scarlet tanagers with their neon red bodies and jet black wings; Honduran indigo buntings with their electric blue figures; Antillean Baltimore orioles whose red-orange plumage defies their blackbird identities; Brazilian yellow warblers so resplendent they challenge the primacy of even the spectacular goldfinches; Jamaican redstarts with their hummingbird-fast, red-orange-black beating wings.

Black bears in their dens; coyotes in the night; foxes and their kits on roadsides; snapping turtles in lakes; raccoons and turkeys and skunks and opossums and red efts and beavers and muskrats and so many more. All confined to an ever-shrinking space by development and pavement, making the Poconos one of the best wildlife viewing areas in all of the United States.

As Herman Melville would say, these preceding paragraphs are but a draft of a draft. In many ways, the nature of my home place is so totalizing and inscrutable that it can never be rendered in words alone. Even if you went there, it wouldn't be the same to you as it is to me. But I can say this with confidence: you'll be amazed by its beauty.

V.

The combination of abandoned resorts and rugged wilderness served as a backdrop to one of the most tragic events that has ever taken place in the Pocono Mountains. On a mid-September night in 2014, Eric Matthew Frein waited outside the Pennsylvania State Trooper barracks in Blooming Grove, armed with a .308 caliber rifle and a violent desire to start a revolution. When the officers conducted a shift change around 11:00pm, Frein opened fire. His bullets struck two unsuspecting and completely defenseless police officers, Corporal Bryon K. Dickson II and Trooper Alex Douglass. Dickson was killed and Douglass sustained life-altering, critical injuries.

Immediately after shooting the two officers, Frein fled into the dense wilderness. He eluded capture for nearly two months. After all, he had planned extensively for this undertaking. In the years before the shooting, he had trained himself in survivalist and paramilitary tactics, even reenacting the ferocious conflicts of Europe's Balkan region. In the days and weeks leading up to the ambush,

Frein had left himself several caches of supplies hidden throughout the Pocono woods. During the manhunt, the very same tracts
of land where we all gathered berries and played carefree amongst
the hammocks of the swamps were closed down for fear that Frein
had squirrelled away firearms and booby-traps. To this day, I cannot help but wonder if one wrong step in the woods of my youth
might lead to my death because of one of Frein's undiscovered pipe
bombs.

The manhunt for Frein reached epic proportions. He was added to the FBI's Ten Most Wanted list. Over a thousand law enforcement officers from around the country participated in the search.
They looked for him by air, on foot, and on the water. All of my
friends and family in the Poconos received knocks on their doors
and requests to search their properties. Cars were stopped continuously. Schools were on a semi-permanent state of lockdown.
An atmosphere of fear and suspicion had taken over the region.
Residents feared going from their houses to their cars, to get the
mail, to take a walk. This is what terrorism is: when you are prevented from living your everyday life because you are afraid you
might be harmed.

They had good reason to be scared. Frein was motivated by a
far-right ideology that seemed to spare no one on the road to revolution. In a letter to his parents that was read out loud during his
trial, Frein wrote: "Our nation is far from what it is and what it
should be. Only passing through the crucible of another revolution
can get us back the liberties we had before." Ordinary people mean
nothing to someone who thinks like this. All was justified in the
name of the revolution he sought to spark.

Frein used the ruggedness of the Pocono woods to his advantage. The very thing that had given birth to the region became
Frein's refuge, further underscoring a lesson I have long come to
learn: the natural world may be beautiful, it may be enchanting and

peaceful and restorative, but it is disinterested and non-agential. It will not take sides in human affairs. And so Frein hid in my native forest and evaded capture there. But even a so-called "survivalist" like him couldn't live off land that rugged forever. It is too harsh; the thorns too sharp, the rocks too many, the nights too cold, the water too swampy, the bears too close, the mosquitoes and gnats too thick. He was bound to come out of it sooner or later.

I watched these events unfold on television from 750 miles away. I like to joke that whenever the Poconos make the national news, it's always for something really horrible. And Frein's was truly a heinous act and the manhunt was incredibly gripping. It is not surprising, then, that CNN and MSNBC and Fox News all carried nightly updates during the 48 day search. I was glued to the TV.

In the early aftermath of the shooting, I told my family and friends that Frein would use the scores of abandoned Pocono resorts as hiding places. And that is exactly what he did.

One day before Halloween, Frein was captured in an abandoned airport hangar that was once part of the Birchwood-Pocono Airpark. I knew Birchwood well, of course – it's only five miles away from my childhood home. It was unique amongst the many places of hospitality in the Poconos because it had its own airport. Those with their own planes could fly there themselves; newlyweds frequently hired private pilots to fly them from New York City to Birchwood so they could celebrate their nuptials in style. It thrived during the halcyon days following the Second World War, when everyone had money and owning your own plane wasn't just reserved for the uber-wealthy. But by the late 90s, Birchwood's business model was no longer sustainable. It closed down when I was a freshman in high school, one of the first ones to go.

And that's where they found Frein. In a place that once welcomed and celebrated young love, where couples disappeared into bedsheets and each other, where new life began and happiness was ubiquitous. Into that sacred and hallowed space a copkiller had come, infecting it with his malevolence and political venom. By the second decade of the new millennium, romance in the Poconos had died a monstrous death.

VI.

But, as this book has endeavored to show, the death of a place isn't always the end of the story. In this case, there's remarkable diversity amid the afterlives of these shuttered resorts and hotels.

Originally formed as a camp for Pennsylvanian socialists, the Tamiment resort hosted tens of thousands of tourists during its nearly 85 year existence. Located about half an hour north of Mountain Manor and the area where I grew up, Tamiment became famous for two things: a gorgeous golf course and a playhouse that earned a reputation for launching careers. Entertainers like Carol Burnett, Woody Allen, and Neil Simon honed their acts on this Pocono stage before making it big. Unlike the conservative Catskill resorts featured in cultural productions like 1987's Dirty Dancing and the recent Amazon Prime hit The Marvelous Mrs. Maisel, Tamiment was more aligned with the countercultures of the 60s and 70s, even featuring swank treehouse-cabins and masquerade balls.

By the mid-2000s, however, Tamiment was sold and the new owners converted many of the old lodgings into rentals, including the treehouses. They also constructed some new sets of condos. During a recent visit there, I saw more cars with New York and New Jersey license plates than Pennsylvania ones. And the resort's once magnificent stone main hall has fallen into disrepair and will likely never be renovated. Tamiment's afterlife is as a strange New York City exurb surrounded by dense Pocono woodland.

Something similar, albeit a little bit different, happened to Buck Hill Falls. Once an egalitarian resort founded by Quakers at the turn of the twentieth century, Buck Hill now describes itself thusly: "Buck Hill Falls is also known as the most exclusive community in the Poconos, and as such, it has remained a sanctuary of family privacy offering a low key-lifestyle of culture and sophistication within its magnificent natural setting." Gentrification at its finest. It makes some sense, though. The original Buck Hill resort was stunningly made: it is mostly comprised out of Pocono rock, with spectacular walls lining the roads and stone bridges that span the area's creeks and horse trails. It is not surprising that the very wealthy scooped up the nicest properties and tore down the rest. They've created quite the tony oasis amid the general impoverishment of my home region. I mean, who wouldn't want to engage in a polite round of lawn bowling on the area's only tournament regulation course? (Hint: not me).

The region's early entrepreneurs worked hard to ensure that the Poconos was a four season destination for travelers. This meant skiing in the wintertime. Usually, ski resorts are quite profitable, but even some of these have begun shutting down in northeastern Pennsylvania. One of the first to close was Alpine Mountain, which was the place where I got my first job at the age of 15.

I hated everything about working there. I was relegated to the kitchen, serving as a Frymaster. After demonstrating my capacity for this kind of work, I was graduated to Wiper of Tables and Cleaner of Bathrooms. Eventually, I became a Cashier in the food court and a Gopherboy to the resort's manager. All of it sucked. One of the stated purposes for this job was to teach me the value of physical labor, or somesuch blue collar sentiment, but in reality all it did was make me that much more determined to go to college and get the fuck out of the Poconos.

But it wasn't without a heavy dose of sadness and nostalgia that I viewed what had become of Alpine Mountain in the spring of 2018. The main road onto the property was gated and covered with about a thousand posted signs, but I decided that I had a right to be there, so I climbed over the gate and walked down the long driveway toward the lodge.

Most of the lodge's windows were broken and vines were growing up the side of the building. The ski slopes behind the lodge were likewise overgrown and the cables of the ski lifts were sagging underneath the weight of still-present chairs. They hung there precariously over the trails that once had names like "Alpine Way" and "Hot Dog." It was like they had just hit the off-switch, left, and then never returned. It was a tough thing to see. So I stood looking at the slopes for a while and mourned not for my time there but for my home and what had happened to it.

Where would the locals work now? Would they fill the void with opiates and alcohol and destroy themselves or would they bravely face the four hour round trip commute to the cities? Would the collapse of the hospitality industry and the regional economy force more people like myself to leave the Poconos for quality educations and jobs? What happens to the towns and cities and school districts without the tax monies that places like Mountain Manor and Alpine Mountain brought in? What happens when an already bad situation gets worse?

VII.

It's not all bad, though. Fernwood – part of which also burned in a suspicious fire – is poised to become a Buddhist meditation center. A friend told me that Alpine Mountain might become an ATV and/or drone park. The Bushkill Inn and Conference Center has been remodeled and is currently open, placing a special emphasis on corporate retreats.

Either changes like these will happen, or the abandoned resorts will further succumb to the elements and be eaten by the forest. It's unlikely that this period of large dilapidated structures will remain much longer. One way or another, they all eventually fall down.

This is what happened to L.W. Brodhead's Kittatinny House. All that remains of it are its stone foundation...and a highway pull-off replete with the name "Resort Overlook." From this parking area, people can gaze out at the view that was once in high demand amongst the elite classes of New York and Philadelphia. Much to Brodhead's chagrin, however, the House's view was blocked from viewing Mount Tammany, the largest peak in the area. The Delaware River turns abruptly through the Water Gap, thereby obscuring the view that Brodhead so coveted. Perhaps it was this disappointment that led to the writing of The Delaware Water Gap: Its Scenery, Its Legends and Early History. To fill a gap left by nature and circumstance, Brodhead created a mythology entirely of his own devising. Fittingly, you can see Princess Winona's waterfall from the current overlook and from the Interstate 80 bridge.

VIII.

It is without dispute that the people of the Pocono Mountains have suffered during these last two decades. Yet, there is a beneficiary to this human catastrophe: the woods of my childhood.

The Great Recession stopped the wide-scale development of the Poconos right in its tracks. Thousands of acres of prime wildlife habitat has been spared. The subsequent years of abandonment have allowed plants to regrow on thousands upon thousands of acres.

Furthermore, several resort properties have now become public open spaces. On the former golf course of the old Penn Hills resort (once under the same ownership as Alpine Mountain), a new park has been opened by Stroud Township. It is called the ForEvergreen Nature Preserve and its primary purpose is to allow a distinct bottomland ecosystem to heal from decades of misuse.

Upon a recent visit there, I was pleasantly surprised to find that the native salmonid, the brook trout, had returned to the waters of the Brodhead Creek. Once the quarry of some of the original visitors of the Poconos, the brookie (as it is called by sportsmen) has been largely extirpated from the region. Before receiving important protections in the preserve, the fish was only found in highland swamps and creeks on the Pocono Plateau. Now a little over a mile of its original range has been restored. While that may seem like a small number in the grand scheme of things, it is nevertheless a significant conservation victory.

Meanwhile, up the mountain near the headwaters of the Bushkill Creek, the former Camp William Penn is now part of the Delaware State Forest. Originally owned and operated by the city of Philadelphia, the camp once hosted hundreds of disadvantaged and underprivileged youth each summer. When I was a child, I would sometimes ride my bike past the camp on the way to some of my favorite trout streams. As I passed by I would listen to the whooping and cheering coming from the fields and the ponds. It always gave me a deep sense of satisfaction to know that inner city children, whose lives were so divorced from nature, could encounter it in all of its Pocono splendor. I still can think of no better place to experience real wilderness for the first time.

Almost all of the Camp's structures – except for one lovely gazebo – have been torn down, dismantled, and removed from the site. The state of Pennsylvania also reseeded the areas where the buildings once stood. Today, you wouldn't even know something was there unless you were acquainted with the history of the property.

Now, whenever I visit the Poconos, I make a point to go to the old Camp William Penn. I have brought my children fishing there, and my wife and I have explored the old graveyard that lies in a wooded copse not far from the big pond. We walk around the fields and look for bobolinks and cattails and redwings and even for the more elusive bears and foxes. Even though I do not live in the Poconos anymore, I am extremely happy that there is a way that my children can roam the exact same woods that I did when I was their age. It is a passing down, an inheritance, a birthright – and it means more to me than I can adequately state.

And this was all made possible by the successful repurposing of a former place of Pocono hospitality. With some care – and a little luck and ingenuity – it is possible to create more spaces like this. Without a doubt, this is the most fitting and appropriate of all the potential afterlives of the lost Pocono resorts.

The People of the Mound

Our nation was formerly very numerous and very powerful; it extended more than twelve days journey from east to west, and more than fifteen from south to north. We reckoned then 500 Suns, and you may judge by that what was the number of the nobles, of the people of rank, and the common people. Now in times past it happened, that one of the two guardians, who were upon duty in the temple, left it on some business, and the other fell asleep, and suffered the fire to go out. When he awaked and saw that he had incurred the penalty of death, he went and got some profane fire, as tho' he had been going to light his pipe, and with that he renewed the eternal fire. His transgression was by that means concealed; but a dreadful mortality immediately ensued, and raged for four years, during which many Suns and an infinite number of the people died.

— Great Sun of the Natchez speaking to Antoine Simon Le Page Du Pratz in "The History of Louisiana"

I.

It may have started with a sniffle, or a cough, or a sneeze; undoubtedly, it began simply enough. But soon it ran through entire communities, transforming hale native bodies into festering vessels of disease. The children – the all-important next generation – were covered in deadly lesions; the strongest of warriors were carried away by fever in a matter of days; the political leadership was rendered breathless by respiratory inflammation – all of this shows that not all genocides are conducted with guns and bombs and gas chambers.

When the bringer of the plagues, the murderous and treacherous Hernando de Soto, moved his expedition through the southeastern section of North America in the middle of the sixteenth century, thousands of Mississippian Indian villages and cities dotted the landscape. At the physical, political, and spiritual center of most of these places were earthen mounds that rival the great pyramids of Egypt and those of the Mayans of Mesoamerica. Millions of people called these mound towns home.

But when Europeans returned in the seventeenth century to these places, they found nothing but ruins and skeletons. I believe that it probably took about a decade – total – to wipe out one of the greatest and most magnificent civilizations to ever exist on this planet. Please let that sink in for a minute.

The destruction of the Mississippian Indian civilization is one of history's greatest tragedies. Yet, most Americans alive today have never heard of these people. What follows is an attempt to bring their experiences to light and to breathe life into one of their many lost places.

II.

I moved to the Blue Ridge Mountains of northern Georgia in the summer of 2014. Before coming down here, I had always lived on land that had once been part of the Lenape civilization. I grew up learning the history of these Algonquian-speaking peoples, who were masters of life along the Delaware River. Never, in any history book, in any museum, or in any textbook, did I ever see anything written about the Mississippians. Chances are, you haven't heard anything about them either. So let me tell you a little bit about them.

The Mississippian civilization thrived in central and eastern North America between the years of 1000 – 1400CE. The people who lived there are known to anthropologists as the Mississippians, though sometimes they are colloquially referred to as "the mound builders." For my money, this is an especially well-earned moniker: indeed, hundreds of Mississippian mounds still exist in the central and southeastern United States. To build something out of materials given only by the earth, and have it survive for more than a millennium is, to me, a testament to the ingenuity, intelligence, and capacity of the ancient human mind. It is nothing short of remarkable.

At the height of their civilization, more Mississippians lived in Cahokia, the largest and most complex of their settlements, than in London or Paris or any other medieval European city. Yet, they remain almost universally unknown. Why is this the case?

I have a few theories. Firstly, if – and this is a very big if – white Americans give any thought at all to the native peoples of the Americas they only think of the groups that were present when colonization happened (as was the case with me), or the ones that are still extant. That is, they think of the Cherokee and the Sioux and the Iroquois, but not of the Paleo peoples or the Woodlanders or the Mississippians. Out of sight and out of mind, right?

Secondly, there seems to be a kind of intentional erasure. The knowledge that there was an advanced civilization in North America replete with complex systems of economy, worship, and engineering at the same time that European capitals were hotbeds of plague, disorder, and war certainly threatens notions of western European dominance and achievement. It also undermines the rationale that European settlement "brought" civilization to the New World.

But despite this purposeful forgetting, the Mississippian civilization did occur – and my, oh my, did it thrive. Its success reached far from Cahokia, into the wilds of the southern Appalachian Mountains. Mississippian towns sprung up along all the major tributaries of the Mississippi River – as well as through southern Georgia and Alabama.

Building their mounds required the entire community's labor. Over and over and over again, the Mississippian peoples would carry baskets of earth to the construction site. Eventually the mounds would reach impressive heights. Furthermore, the mounds were also always already being built; they were constantly being added to, buttressed, or even reduced in certain situations. They were active, living structures, true symbols of community identity.

Because of this complex and perpetual building ritual, each person had a personal investment in the mounds. Not surprisingly, the Mississippians used their mounds for a variety of purposes. For some, they served as platforms on which wooden structures were erected – often, a political leader would construct his home on top of a mound. Sometimes they buried their dead in the mounds, especially in the more northern reaches of their empire. Still other mounds seemed strategically oriented according to concepts of urban design. Sites of political power, sites of mourning, sites of urbanity. The mounds were the center of Mississippian life.

The presence of these magnificent earthen structures also indicates that the Mississippians lived in permanent settlements, unlike the native peoples who inhabited the earlier Woodland, Archaic and Paleo eras. And although the Mississippians weren't the first humans to come to the southeastern United States, they were the first to settle there for good. Accordingly, this means that the Mississippians were the first people to be displaced from the region.

So what happened to them? As any archaeologist worth her salt would tell you, civilizational collapse usually doesn't happen for any one reason. But in this case, the diseases introduced by the de Soto expedition were the primary agents for the destruction of the Mississippian people. Add on to that something like the following: climate change of some sort likely led to trouble with the annual maize crop, these food shortages led to societal discord, which eventually led to warfare and the wide-scale abandonment of the mound settlements. Some fractured groups of Mississippians were still present when the first Europeans explored North America, particularly the Natchez in Louisiana. Predictably, this contact led to further epidemics and the eventual end of the culture entirely.

III.

As previous passages in this book indicate, my favorite pastime is fly fishing for trout. So soon after moving to the Blue Ridge, I began investigating the tailwater streams that flow out of the large Tennessee Valley Authority hydroelectric dams in the region. My closest tailwater is the Hiwassee River, which is created by releases from the Chatuge Dam in Clay County, North Carolina. Access to the river is difficult, since most of it is surrounded by private property. A gorgeous stretch of it, however, is on public land owned by the town of Hayesville. Several years ago, I took a walk with my wife and daughters from the Clay County Recreation Center back to the banks of the Hiwassee. Along the way, we passed by a Mississippian mound. Ever since then, I've researched, read, looked around, searched the riverbank, riverbed and adjacent fields, spoke with anthropologists, and visited other mound complexes – all to try to arrive at an understanding of what life was like in this particular lost place.

What are the results of my labors? Well, even the simplest of my questions remain unanswered, like: what was the mound town called? We know that when white settlers came through the area in the eighteenth century there was a Cherokee trading village located by the Hayesville mound. The Cherokee called this place Quanassee. However, the Cherokee had only lived there for a short period, were not the builders of the mound, and therefore had no inherited knowledge of the former inhabitants.

By way of contrast, the Mississippians lived there for centuries, and archaeological evidence that I've analyzed suggests that their ancestors had lived there for at least a thousand years before them (it's almost certainly more than this). Yet, if you go to Hayesville, you'll find an exhibit dedicated to the Cherokee. You'll find signs and information near the mound that speak about the Cherokee. If you ask the old timers what Indians lived there and built the mound, every last one of them would answer: "the Cherokee."

Part of the problem is that the Mississippians only had a rudimentary form of writing, so they left little self-authored materials behind. The discipline of archaeology is certainly one way of combating this problem, but to my dismay I learned that the mound in Hayesville has received scant study from scholars. No one has conducted a dig or done any field research at the site for decades. Part of the reason for this comes from the continued assault on higher education. Archaeology and anthropology are two of the most adversely affected disciplines in the current higher education crisis. When schools are pressed for money and need to clear space in their budgets, these are the positions that are often the first to go.

One day, sitting beside the mound and staring out at the beautiful river, I had a realization: no one was coming. It dawned on me that if anyone was going to study these people and attempt to tell their story, well, it had to be me - an English professor with literally zero archaeological knowledge. As this book demonstrates, though, I am a trained historian with the ability to process complex information and develop narratives out of it. The Mississippian peoples of the Hayesville mound clearly deserve a smart and capable archaeologist; however, they're stuck with me. All things considered, I think it could be worse.

IV.

Archaeological evidence from the Hayesville site indicates that the mound was likely constructed at some point between 1000-1300CE. Furthermore, the town's population likely peaked in the high hundreds between 1300-1600CE. It is important to note that this lost place's heyday occurred before contact with European explorers and settlers – and that the subsequent contact was what lead to its demise.

There is no mention of this particular mound village in the various records of the de Soto expedition. That being said, we do know that the area surrounding the Hiwassee River watershed was part of the broader Coosa Chiefdom (rendered Coça in the de Soto accounts). Mississippian civilization was divided thusly. Each mound site had a leader called a Sun who oversaw spiritual and political life in his town. Each Sun was subordinate to a regional leader called a Great Sun or a paramount chief. In this case, the Sun of the Hayesville mound gave his allegiance to the leader of the Coosa Chiefdom.

In a classically despicable move, Hernando de Soto took the Great Sun of the Coosa captive in the year 1540. The Coosa people did not take this lightly, but their resistance was, indeed, futile. Consider the following passage from an account of de Soto's expedition:

The men of Coça seeing their lord detained, took it in evil part, and revolted, and hid themselves in the woods, as well those of the town of the cacique, as those of the other towns of his principal subjects. The Governor sent out four captains, every one his way, to seek them. They took many men and women, which were put into chains. They seeing the hurt which they received, and how little they gained in absenting themselves, came again, promising to do whatsoever they were commanded. Of those which were taken prisoners, some principal men were set at liberty, whom the cacique demanded; and every one that had any, carried the rest in chains like slaves, without letting them go to their country. Neither did any return, but some few, whose fortune helped them with the good diligence which they used to file off their chains by night, or such as in their traveling could slip aside out of the way, seeing any negligence in them that kept them; some escaped away with the chains, and with the burdens and clothes which they carried.

Such was de Soto's modus operandi. Taking the Great Suns captive enabled him to compel allegiance from the lower ranking Suns in the surrounding villages. His firepower and horses meant that Mississippian rebellions were easily put down. So the de Soto men came into the Coosa Chiefdom and kidnapped its leader, stole its food, looted its precious metals, and in all likelihood, raped and murdered Coosa women. On top of all of this, of course, was the spread of measles and smallpox to the natives, who had no natural immunities to the maladies. As I mentioned at the beginning of this chapter, it took less than a decade for these diseases to destroy the entire Mississippian civilization, the Hayesville mound site included.

After more than two month's captivity, de Soto finally released the Great Sun of Coosa – after he had taken him all the way to present day Tuscaloosa, Alabama. De Soto would go on to inflict massive damage everywhere he went, before finally succumbing to what might have been malaria on the banks of the Mississippi River. Years after the start of the expedition, only about 300 men made it out alive.

What they did was unspeakable; it was true, absolute, abject horror. I wish they all would have died.

V.

Though the Hayesville mound town gave its political loyalty to the Coosa, its cultural allegiance was directed at another place: Etowah. Located near present day Cartersville, Georgia, Etowah was a magnificent Mississippian city, replete with some of the largest mounds ever constructed in the Western Hemisphere. It is thankfully preserved today as a Georgia State Park. I highly recommend visiting if you ever find yourself in the Atlanta area. It's a breathtaking place.

Several hundred years ago, during the peak of the Hayesville mound town, Etowah was an artistic powerhouse. Its denizens produced and exported clothing, jewelry, ceramics, and religious iconography throughout the entire southeast. And, if a Mississippian artwork wasn't made in Etowah, chances are very good that it was inspired by the artistic traditions born there.

Etowah's influence on the Hayesville site is perhaps most saliently illustrated through pottery. Indeed, the Mississippians were master potters. They made water jugs, cooking pots, pipes, bowls, plates, and much more. All of these various ceramics were covered in gorgeous designs. Most of the sherds recovered near the Hayesville mound are stamped with flowing lines, circles, and studded rims. They made these vessels in part from the sand of the Hiwassee River, which contains countless semi-precious gemstones like garnets. To this day, if you hold a piece of their pottery in the sun, it still sparkles like the day it was made. I don't think I've ever seen any objects that are more beautiful.

Even more so than the spectacular mounds they left behind, their stunning pottery was what drew me into the world of the Mississippians and served as the inspiration for this chapter. One day a few years ago, I stood in the cool water of the Hiwassee, right in the shadow of the mound. I was casting dry flies to rising wild rainbow trout when something glimmering from the riverbed caught my eye. I bent down and reached into the water, expecting to pick up a piece of mica (itself a favorite among the Mississippians). Instead it was a broken piece of ancient pottery, full of shining garnets. It had straight lines running next to each other in small squares, with gentle curving lines interspersed throughout. I later was able to identify it as a piece of Lamar complicated stamped pottery – perhaps the most common pottery type found near Mississippian settlements.

Since that day, my family and I have found many more pottery shards, including some beautiful rim pieces. One time, about a year ago, my four year old daughter stood next to me while I was fishing. I turned to look at her and she was holding a pottery sherd that was four inches long and three inches wide – still the largest piece any of us have found. "Look what I found, daddy," she said. There's nothing quite like watching your little kid find an eight-hundred year old cultural relic.

Above all else, the Mississippian ceramic artifacts that I've encountered near the Hayesville mound site facilitate a kind of remembering. It's not my memory, per se – but Morrisonian "re-memory" once again. Through the pottery sherds left behind by these ancient peoples, I am able to access – or at least come into contact with – their rememories. The Mississippians are thus not dead, not forgotten, not left behind.

Here, I'll turn to the words of Paul Ricoeur, one of the world's leading philosophers of memory. In his seminal book, Memory, History, Forgetting, Ricoeur says this:

It is indeed at this primordial level that the phenomenon of "memory places" is constituted, before they become a reference for historical knowledge. These memory places function for the most part after the manner of reminders, offering in turn support for fail-ing memory, a struggle in the war against forgetting, even the silent plea of dead memory. These places "remain" as inscriptions, mon-uments, potentially as documents, whereas memories transmitted only along the oral path fly away as do the words themselves.

The memory of life at the Hayesville mound has been imbued into these pottery sherds. Touching them thus produces a resurrec-tion. In my mind's eye I see a young woman – a new bride, perhaps – touching the cool clay, softly molding it into form. I see her take a stylus, one made from the antler of a white-tailed deer, and carve her beautiful designs into it. As she delicately traces the lines and curves into the flesh of the pot, she is reminded of her mother, who taught her this art. Once finished, she takes the wet vessel and plac-es it in a pit in the ground, surrounding it with smoldering coals. She covers the pit with a slab of sandstone and walks away. While she waits, she rearranges the rose quartz decorations in the window of her hut, grinds some maize, and repairs a patch of her cane roof. When the right amount of time has passed, she returns to the pit and extracts her masterpiece. Once it cools, she'll fill it with clean, cool water from a nearby spring. Later, perhaps years down the line, she'll make a mistake and drop her water jug; or perhaps her child will carelessly knock it from its perch. It'll shatter, but she won't be sad. She'll throw the broken pieces into the river, gather more clay, and begin the process anew.

I can see her clearly, and I know her. She's real. She's not forgotten. Her rememory lives on in my mind, at the mound near Hayesville, and in the pages of this book. I would like for you to remember her, too.

VI.

On a warm spring day, just weeks before the coronavirus pandemic shut down American life, I sat next to the Hiwassee River near the Hayesville mound. From a distance I could hear the classic signs of American spring: the sound of metal bats striking baseballs, the shouts of the coaches desperately trying to teach children the mechanics of the game, car honks as people came and went. The humanmade sounds were blended with the noise of mating frogs, chipper kingfishers, and the buzz of honeybees. It was a cacophony that made me happy to be in that place, at that time.

I looked at the mound and thought of the Mississippians. They, too, played a rousing game, one called chunkey. Here is how it is described by Antoine Simon Le Page Du Pratz in his "The History of Louisiana":

The warriors practise a diversion which is called the game of the pole, at which only two play together at a time. Each has a pole about eight feet long, resembling a Roman f, and the game consists in rolling a flat round stone, about three inches diameter and an inch thick, with the edge somewhat sloping, and throwing the pole at the same time in such a manner, that when the stone rests, the pole may touch it or be near it. Both antagonists throw their poles at the same time, and he whose pole is nearest the stone counts one, and has the right of rolling the stone. The men fatigue themselves much at this game, as they run after their poles at every throw; and some of them are so bewitched by it, that they game away one piece of furniture after another.

Le Page lived with the Natchez tribe for eight years. His description of them is thus the account of native peoples who practiced the Mississippian cultural tradition. The above narration of the chunkey sport is likely quite accurate – it is very much how the people of the Hayesville mound would have played their favorite game.

That spring day I imagined Mississippian men and boys throwing spears at the discoidal disc until they were exhausted, with their wives and children cheering them on. I was struck by how similar the scene in my mind's eye was to the action taking place on the baseball diamond a short distance away.

The Mississippians may be a lost people, victims of a horrific series of epidemics. They may not have written much, and only the Natchez still followed their way of life into the eighteenth century. But they were still people, just like us. They played games and people watched. They felt the pride of victory, and the frustration of defeat. They taught their children how to play. On and on it goes. One human story after another after another.

They also made gorgeous clothing and jewelry. Indeed, they were specialists working with the medium of copper. The people of the mound near Hayesville would have been positioned well with respect to this element. The mountains in the Hiwassee River watershed contain several veins of copper. Materials made from this substance were traded for things in short supply, such as ocean shells. Copper beads, earrings, necklaces, and crown-like objects have all been found at various Mississippian archaeological sites. Americans today wear gold and silver; the Mississippians wore copper.

They celebrated holidays, holding festivals that roughly followed what we would call months. Most of these were based upon the availability of food. For the Mississippians, the year started in spring, as is common with many indigenous peoples in northern, seasonal climates. Their first holiday was that of the deer, a readily available resource all winter long. Then, they celebrated the strawberry, which was followed by their first corn harvest. As the spring gave way to the summer, they would gather and celebrate melons, then fish, then wild berries. In the late fall and throughout the winter, they centered festivals on wild turkeys, buffalo, bears, ground maize, chestnuts, and finally walnuts.

It was in the beginning of fall, however, that they held their most important and largest celebration. Much like many rural American communities do to this day, the Mississippians reaped their maize fields and held a community-wide feast. I'll let le Page describe the end of this most important of Mississippian celebrations:

This great solemnity is concluded with a general dance by torch-light. Upwards of two hundred torches of dried canes, each of the thickness of a child, are lighted round the place, where the men and women often continue dancing till day-light; and the following is the disposition of their dance. A man places himself on the ground with a pot covered with a deer-skin, in the manner of a drum, to beat time to the dances; round him the women form themselves into a circle, not joining hands, but at some distance from each other; and they are inclosed by the men in another circle, who have in each hand a chichicois, or calabash, with a stick thrust through it to serve for a handle. When the dance begins, the women move round the men in the centre, from left to right, and the men contrariwise from right to left, and they sometimes narrow and sometimes widen their circles. In this manner the dance continues without intermission the whole night, new performers successively taking the place of those who are wearied and fatigued.

An all-night, community dance. Bellies full of life-giving corn. Deep, rich, and gorgeous rituals. It all sounds absolutely wonderful. It is an immense tragedy that it's gone.

VII.

It's important to note that the Mississippian civilization was not some kind of utopia (human societies, big and small, never are). Their history is littered with examples of violent conflict, economic inequality, torture, and even human sacrifice.

After serious attempts at diplomacy failed, it was sometimes the case that various Mississippian groups fought wars with each other. Indeed, even Cahokia, with its huge population, felt insecure enough to build a wooden wall around itself. They had good reason to do so.

According to the Le Page account of the Natchez, the Mississippians regularly engaged in the torture of captive enemies. First, the winning side tied its prisoners of war up to a sturdy set of river canes. Then, in front of the whole village, the warriors would commence their torture. Here's how Le Page describes it:

The young men in the mean time having prepared several bundles of canes, set fire to them; and several of the warriors taking those flaming canes, burn the prisoner in different parts of his body, while others burn him in other parts with their tobacco-pipes. The patience of prisoners in those miserable circumstances is altogether astonishing. No cries or lamentations proceed from them; and some have been known to suffer tortures, and sing for three days and nights without intermission.

Despite the barbarity of this practice, there existed a fascinating mechanism that could bring about the end of the torture. A woman who had lost her husband in the conflict could declare an end to the ordeal and select a new husband from the captive population. The man would be freed and would immediately become a member of the winning tribe.

This follows the general human desire for fairness: "if I lose my spouse and primary provider of money, food, protection, etc. to war, I may offset this loss by gaining a new one." It also serves to strengthen ties between the warring factions, thereby reducing the likelihood of additional conflict. That the women were the ones to instigate this practice of conflict resolution should come as no surprise. I immediately think of Aristophanes' comedy Lysistrata, in which the women of various Greek city-states hatch a plan to stop the Peloponnesian War by withholding sex from the men. It seems to me that, in societies in which the participants of war are all men and women are dependent on men for economic and literal survival (both of these were the case with the Mississippians and the Greeks), women would have a rational reason for trying to prevent war, or at least mitigate the effects of it. And that seems to be what's behind this fascinating cultural practice.

As the above paragraph indicates, the Mississippian civilization was characterized by significant inequality. It wasn't just confined to differences in standing between men and women, either. In fact, much of their inequality was class-based.

Economists, historians, sociologists, and anthropologists alike have posited various theories for why inequality exists in human societies. My thoughts on this issue are informed by the thinking of evolutionary biologists like E.O. Wilson, economists like Karl Marx, and philosophers like Friedrich Nietzsche. To me, inequality is a natural outcome of complex human societies. Once survival begins to fade into the background of everyday life because of innovations like agriculture, architecture, cooking technologies, etc. human populations inevitably explode. Then, instead of everyone working toward a common goal of community survival (since this has been effectively solved), humans begin to compete over the resources produced by their group's success. The winners of this competition tend to become the political leaders of the group. These leaders then form dynastic lineages that can last for thousands of years. This is the case everywhere around the world, from the great Egyptian civilizations, to imperial Japan, to the feudal days of England, to the Mayans and Incas and yes, the Mississippians.

Importantly, unequal societies almost always have a way for people to move from one class to the other. The price can be quite steep. In contemporary America, if one wishes to move from the lower, working classes, the best way to do so is to take out student loans to pay for one's college education. In the United States, as of this writing, there exists over 1.5 trillion dollars of student loan debt. Quite a lot, indeed.

In Mississippian societies, the price could be paid in blood. One of the most harrowing moments in Le Page's account of the Natchez comes when the Great Sun's brother – his chief warrior and military leader named Stung Serpent – suddenly died. Stung Serpent had an enormous household that he supported, including multiple wives and servants. All of these were to be sacrificed and buried along with him (except for his children, the sparing of whom enabled his genetic line to continue forward).

The way Stung Serpent's dependents were killed speaks to the bloody means by which Mississippians could move up their society's social ladder. Consider this moment narrated by Le Page: "Those who were appointed to die were conducted twice a day, and placed in two rows before the temple, where they acted over the scene of their death, each accompanied by eight of their own relations who were to be their executioners, and by that office exempted themselves from dying upon the death of any of the Suns, and likewise raised themselves to the dignity of men of rank." Killed by their own families, Stung Serpent's household members' deaths enabled their relatives to move from lower to higher ranks.

People from outside Stung Serpent's household also engaged in this practice. Here, again, is a passage from Le Page: "A child... had been strangled...by its father and mother, which ransomed their lives upon the death of the Great Sun, and raised them from the rank of Stinkards to that of Nobles." In this case, members of the lowest class in Natchez society – the Stinkards, as Le Page calls them – were able to purchase their way into higher societal position by sacrificing their own child.

As Stung Serpent's funeral procession began, the parents of the dead child threw it on the ground in front of the marchers. Then, those who were selected to die and be buried with Stung Serpent were strangled by their relatives. All were buried together and Stung Serpent's hut was ritualistically burned.

As awful as this all seems, it, once again, makes a degree of rational sense. Left alive, Stung Serpent's huge household would have to be dispersed out into the community, thereby putting a significant strain on those who took them in. Furthermore, the parents of the sacrificed child could rationally think to themselves: "well, if we sacrifice this one child, we will move up in society and can therefore provide more resources to our future and/or other children, who will themselves become people of high ranking."

It must have been worth it in their eyes. Otherwise, how else can we explain their readiness to commit these acts?

VIII.

The previous passages will surely sicken some of you. I understand your outrage, I really do – I have felt it at times myself. However, I caution you to withhold your judgements of these people. They lived under a different set of historical, social, and environmental circumstances, with an entirely different moral code. It is thus a fool's errand to judge the people of the past by the standards of your own moment.

And besides, it's not like citizens of the United States in 2020 (or that of the world) are really in any position to judge the Mississippians. Right now, we are witnessing massive protests against police brutality and systemic racism playing out on the streets of our major cities and our smallest towns; we have been at war "against terrorism" for more than half of my life; migrant children are being separated from their families and "lost" at our southern border; and the gap between the haves and the have-nots continues to grow.

All of that, combined with the actions of our European ancestors with respect to the native peoples like the Mississippians, leaves us with little moral ground to stand upon.

As brutal and cruel as their actions may seem, it is quite possible – indeed even likely – that they knew better than we do.

IX.

The mound in Hayesville has become a home away from home for my family and me. My children have learned to fly kites by it, to fish for trout in the river that cuts along its base, and to learn about the people who once called it home. Every time we go to this spot, I remind my children of the original inhabitants. I always try to honor and remember them.

Humans are bad at this. We think that we are the only ones who have ever existed or the only ones that matter. We are very much creatures of the here and now. Learning about deep history and the peoples of the past requires introspection and a sense of one's smallness and insignificance. These aren't easy lessons to learn, but they are of the utmost importance. There very well may come a day when all that's left of our lives are the artifacts we leave behind and the memories we imprint in the landscape. We are all destined to become ghosts in the wind.

Knowing that the ground we tread was once home to the people of a lost civilization also speaks to the impermanence of human societies. The story of the Mississippians teaches us that we should not take our current moment for granted. It may all fall apart in a heartbeat.

However, what I'm left with at the end of this story is a simple feeling of awe. The people of the mound in Hayesville were incredible. They made beautiful art. They played beautiful games. They built magnificent structures. They lived and laughed and loved and did all the wonderful things that happy and flourishing human beings do. And though their way of life and their very lives were taken from them, I know they're still here, waiting for us to discover them, to learn from them, and to honor them.

So I say this to the people of the mound: thank you for all you've taught me. I'm a better person because of you.

"…circles and circles of sorrow": Willard, Virginia

"In that place, where they tore the nightshade and blackberry patches from their roots to make room for the Medallion City Golf Course, there was once a neighborhood. It stood in the hills above the valley town of Medallion and spread all the way to the river. It is called the suburbs now, but when black people lived there it was called the Bottom."

— Toni Morrison, *Sula*

I.

I can imagine what the white people said:

"An airport, sure. We do need an airport. But here? Where we live?"

"Why not put it someplace else?"

"How about somewhere further out, where there are less people."

And, inevitably:

"What about over where the Black folks live? You know, out toward Chantilly."

"What's that Black town called? Willard or something like that?"

"Yeah – Willard. They should put the airport in Willard."

And that's exactly what they did. After initially choosing Burke, Virginia – a largely white and affluent suburb of Washington D.C. – the federal government changed course and decided to construct what ultimately became Dulles International Airport on top of what was once the town of Willard. At least 100 people, almost all of whom were Black, were displaced to make way for this major infrastructural project.

Today, over twenty million people fly in and out of Dulles annually; indeed, its proximity to the power center of D.C. makes it one of the busiest and most important airports in the world. And if you were to ask each one of these twenty million people what was once located on the same tract of land as the airport, I'm willing to bet that not even one of them would know the answer.

The story of Willard, though, helps show just how much of the modern United States was built upon the suffering of poor communities of color. It also demonstrates how histories of this nature, the ones that poke holes in the mythic concept of the American Dream and the country's founding ideals, are themselves bulldozed and buried.

Where there is now an airport a neighborhood once existed. And although it is now gone, it is possible to reconstruct it, to contextualize it, to place it down in words. This is exactly what Toni Morrison does in her novel *Sula*, in which she describes the fate of a fictional Black community called the Bottom, which was displaced to make room for a golf course. As Morrison writes,

...it wasn't a town anyway: just a neighborhood where on quiet days people in valley houses could hear singing sometimes, banjos sometimes, and if a valley man happened to have business up in those

hills – collecting rent or insurance payments – he might see a dark
woman in a flowered dress doing a bit of cakewalk, a bit of black bot-
tom, a bit of 'messing around' to the lively notes of a mouth organ.
Her bare feet would raise the saffron dust that floated down on the
coveralls and bunion-split shoes of the man breathing music in and
out of his harmonica.

And this is what Willard was too: an American place full of
human life, disrupted and destroyed. As I've already point out in
this book, what white people want, white people get. That, too, is
the story of Willard, Virginia.

II.

The history of Black people in the United States and its former
colonies is one long story of displacement. This is not, at all, an
exaggeration. Allow me to explain.

It all began with the kidnapping of millions of Africans,
most of whom lived in the western part of that huge continent.
According to the Trans-Atlantic Slave Trade database, over 12.5
million people were abducted from their homes and sold into international slavery. 12.5 million people! That's more human beings
than currently live in the countries of Sweden, Switzerland, and
The Gambia. It's a number that is so high and so abjectly horrible
that it is hard for the mind to comprehend.

So, if we trace the history of Black America back to its origin
point, this is what we find: human beings snatched from their
homes, from their parents, from their loved ones, from their home
places.

Here's how Olaudah Equiano, one of the most accomplished African American writers of the eighteenth century, described his abduction:

One day, when all our people were gone out to their works as usual, and only I and my dear sister were left to mind the house, two men and a woman got over our walls, and in a moment seized us both, and, without giving us time to cry out, or make resistance, they stopped our mouths, and ran off with us into the nearest wood. Here they tied our hands, and continued to carry us as far as they could, till night came on, when we reached a small house, where the robbers halted for refreshment, and spent the night.

Equiano was carried from town to town, separated from his sister, and sold repeatedly, until he eventually arrived at a port city on the coast. There, he was loaded onto a slave ship and brought to the New World along with several hundred other Africans. Before he even left Africa, he was displaced perhaps a dozen different times! That's how Equiano and three hundred thousand other Africans began their American experience.

It took two to three months to complete the ocean journey from Africa to North America. During this time, the newly minted slaves were subjected to horrific conditions in the hulls of the slave ships. Slave ship captains were under orders to fit as many people as they could into their boats. Of course, each person represented profit for the capitalist owners of these shipping enterprises (which, in the case of the country of Brazil, were state-funded businesses). So the more slaves they could stuff into the squalid conditions below deck, the more money they could all make.

The Middle Passage, as it was called, resulted in the deaths of millions of human beings. I cannot emphasize the following point enough: people are simply not meant to be packed into tight spaces on boats for months at a time. It destroys their health. They become ill with pathogens (introduced from the white sailors), become infected with various bacteria like e.coli from having to live in their own shit and piss, lose their will to live, and have their mental health absolutely decimated. Women and girls were subjected to rape and other horrific abuses. Not surprisingly, the aforementioned database estimates that around two and a half million Africans died in transit. For these individuals, the final act of displacement came when the seamen threw their lifeless bodies overboard. The seabed of the Atlantic Ocean is lined with the displaced corpses of Africans.

Upon arrival, slaves were brought to cities like New Orleans or Savannah. There, they were paraded in front of slaveowners eager for new labor, slavetraders who filled the roles of middle men, and general opportunists looking to make a quick dollar. It was at this point – the slave auction – that families who had managed to stay together during the Middle Passage were torn asunder.

Here's a description of a slave auction held near Edenton, North Carolina. The writer is Harriet Jacobs, a slave woman who hid in a crawlspace to avoid the sexual advances of her master for over seven years. Listen to the horror inherent in this passage:

On one of these sale days, I saw a mother lead seven children to the auction-block. She knew that some of them would be taken from her; but they took all. The children were sold to a slave-trader, and their mother was bought by a man in her own town. Before night her children were all far away. She begged the trader to tell her where he intended to take them; this he refused to do. How could he, when he knew he would sell them, one by one, wherever he could command the highest price? I met that mother in the street, and her wild, haggard face lives to-day in my mind. She wrung her hands in anguish, and exclaimed, "Gone! All gone! Why don't God kill me?" I had no words wherewith to comfort her. Instances of this kind are of daily, yea, of hourly occurrence.

I'm with Harriet. I have no words either.

Once brought to a plantation or a coastal city, slaves were always subjected to resale. At any moment, the capriciousness of their owners could lead them to be displaced again and again. Constantly, the threat of being ripped from place to place existed in their minds. I, personally, find it hard to even fathom such cruelty. I do not know how anyone could stand to know that their children could be taken from them at any time, for any reason. What a menacing and horrible threat that must have been.

Of course, after slavery was ended there were several Back-To-Africa Movements in the United States. Not content to simply allow former slaves to live in the country that they had literally made with their labor, white Americans sought again to displace Black people. This time, they wanted to send them back to Africa! And they did! The whole country of Liberia was founded under this principle. The US set up a colony in Africa in which it could place its unwanted free Black population. Over 10,000 African Americans were sent there.

During the Reconstruction-era, many Black Americans fled the South and the rising power of the Ku Klux Klan for industrial cities in the North. This was not something that these people did because they wanted to; they were forced from their Southern homes by the terroristic tactics of "defeated" Confederates. The so-called Great Migration is one of the more understudied incidences of displacement of African Americans in American history.

Things did not improve during the Jim Crow Era at the end of the nineteenth century and the dawn of the twentieth century. During this period, a large number of Black Americans began moving closer and closer to cities, like the people who came to live in Willard, Virginia. Here's how W.E.B. Dubois describes this phenomenon:

Besides this, the chance for lawless oppression and illegal exactions is vastly greater in the country than in the city, and nearly all the more serious race disturbances of the last decade have arisen from disputes in the count between master and man,—as, for instance, the Sam Hose affair. As a result of such a situation, there arose, first, the Black Belt; and, second, the Migration to Town. The Black Belt was not, as many assumed, a movement toward fields of labor under more genial climatic conditions; it was primarily a huddling for self-protection,—a massing of the black population for mutual defence in order to secure the peace and tranquillity necessary to economic advance. This movement took place between Emancipation and 1880, and only partially accomplished the desired results. The rush to town since 1880 is the counter-movement of men disappointed in the economic opportunities of the Black Belt.

As Dubois makes clear, Black people were making the move to places like Willard not because they wanted to, but because they were forced to. It was yet another example of displacement in this exhausting and terribly long list.

And this is where we find the people of Willard in the early 1950s, just a few years before the gigantic airport construction project would upend Black lives once again.

III.

There's nothing particularly notable about Willard; it was, in many ways, a quintessential American small town.

Only about 100 people lived there, most of whom were members of a few Black families. I have been able to find some of their names: Eldridge Smith, Nathaniel Corum, Joseph Holmes, and

Charles Newman. In the early twentieth century, these men and their wives and children lived quiet, agrarian lives. They grew their own food, worked their own land, and performed jobs on large farms nearby for extra money. It really was a peaceable, quiet existence.

That part of Northern Virginia where Willard was located was still the hinterlands from 1900-1950. The nation's capital, located down the road, had not yet taken on the gargantuan proportions that it enjoys today. The District – as it was known to those who lived near Willard – might as well have been as far away as Paris or London.

The Black families of Willard all lived together because Jim Crow laws prevented them from living in white communities (and as Dubois points out, for protection). The Plessy vs. Ferguson ruling in the late 1800s ensured that white people could legally discriminate against Black people, and, as the suburbs around D.C. continued to grow, Black families were continuously denied access to these spaces and places. Thus the people of Willard stayed in Willard.

They worshipped at the Shiloh Primitive Baptist Church. Ever since their introduction to the New World through the Middle Passage, many African Americans have embraced their own version of Christianity. Even by the middle of the 1700s, Black congregations had sprouted up all throughout the colonies of North America. A principal motivation was to maintain a religious experience for Black people by Black people. This tradition continues to this day at AME churches all over the United States. For the people of Willard, it meant listening to circuit preachers who ministered to the many different Black communities in the Northern Virginia area.

Life stayed more or less the same in Willard until the dawn of the aviation age. And after the white residents of Burke got their way, the federal government turned its eyes to this small little Black town.

It used the same tactics it had used in the Smoky Mountains and would later come to use in the Valley of the Minisink: notably, condemnation. Keep in mind, if a home was condemned, its owners received far less money than if it was subjected to eminent domain. And since all the landowners in Willard were Black, the government just steamrolled them into submission. Their properties were condemned, they received a pittance, their homes were bulldozed, and they were forced to relocate.

To reiterate: what white people want, white people get. And what they wanted in this case was a gigantic airport, one that would be built on Black land, not white land. And so today we have Dulles International Airport.

IV.

I thought for a while that the church might still exist. Often, when these projects develop and communities are faced with displacement, the authorities at least move their churches for them. Think of the scene at the end of the movie Deliverance, in which the town of Aintry's church is put on wheels and moved to a new location. Not so in Willard.

There is evidence that the government did move the graveyard, however. So much like the deceased Africans who were jettisoned from slave ships during the Middle Passage, Willard's dead were subjected to a final act of displacement.

I set out on a very cold January day to try to find where the government moved these people. After much searching (and quite a few U-turns), I think I was successful.

Emphasis on the "think."

Nothing else better represents the callous disregard for the Black families of Willard, Virginia than the fact that one cannot say with certainty where the government of the United States moved the bodies of the dead to make way for a fucking airport. If you are Black in America, you are rarely allowed to rest in peace.

V.

I've spent a lot of time in Northern Virginia. After all, it's where my wife and her family are from. We thus visit the area multiple times each year. To me – a child of the Appalachian Mountains – this conglomeration of suburbs and exurbs and cities and shopping malls and gridlocked roads is pandemonium squared. Its constant, dizzying speed is, for me, its defining feature. It is truly a whirlwind of motion.

According to the Northern Virginia Regional Commission, the area houses over 2.5 million people and is "one of the fastest growing and most diverse communities in the United States." This manifests itself in towering apartment complexes, regional railway lines, and traffic from your worst nightmares. But it also means that you are surrounded by a kaleidoscope of diversity.

In fact, the area is nearing minority-majority status. The two biggest drivers of this change are Hispanic Americans and Asian Americans. Indeed, a wonderful Korean grocery store has opened near my in-laws' house. It is full of incredibly rich ingredients, including the best seafood section I have ever seen in any store in America. And, because it is Northern Virginia, the patrons of the store are not just Korean Americans. I've seen customers there that represent pretty much every ethnic group you can possibly think of.

It is quite ironic – and lovely – to see a thriving, multiracial community existing on land that used to be part of the Confederate States of America. Nevertheless, you can still find vestiges of this lost history if you look closely enough.

Until very recently (as in the year of this writing), one regional high school changed its name from Robert E. Lee High to John R. Lewis High. It is a testament to the staying power of the Confederate legacy that such a change only came after the racial reckoning that rocked the US after George Floyd's murder in the summer of 2020.

Perhaps more pertinent to this chapter is Sully Plantation, a historic property located...on the grounds of Dulles Airport. In what can only be described as a direct slap in the face of the displaced Black residents of Willard, Sully Plantation was acquired by the federal government when it decided to construct Dulles near Chantilly. Unlike the Black town of Willard, the defunct plantation – owned for centuries by members of the Lee family who literally fought for the perpetual enslavement of Black people – was given protected status. No parking lot was built over it, no terminal constructed on it, no runway covering it, nothing. White people donated thousands of dollars to fix it up. You can still go and visit it, if you'd like.

To reiterate. The United States of America changed the planned location of this D.C. area airport after white residents of Burke, Virginia complained about its proposed location. The government then moved on to a spot that included a Black town with over 100 residents. It displaced them all without giving them fair value for their homes, and left behind no record of the disinterment of the town's cemetery. It did all this WHILE PRESERVING A FORMER PLANTATION ON WHICH GENERATIONS OF BLACK AMERICANS WERE ENSLAVED. I don't know what else to say.

VI.

I've only flown in and out of Dulles one time. I had a conference to attend in London and my wife and I decided it would be better for her and our infant child to spend that week with her family in Northern Virginia. So I drove us from the Blue Ridge of North Georgia up to Annandale, Virginia and then hopped on a plane bound for the United Kingdom.

At the time, I had no idea about the history of the airport. That's fitting, really, since almost no one knows the racist legacy that led to Dulles being placed in that exact spot. It's the kind of thing that vanishes.

I wish I could author some moving lines about the power of international travel and the ways by which the commercial aviation industry has changed the world. Even though this is all true, I honestly don't really care. To me, Dulles is just another boring and vaguely menacing airport. Everything is asphalt and concrete, there's a ton of traffic in and out, the toll road you have to take to get there requires extra money to traverse, and the restaurants kind of suck. The planes that land there circle overhead, flying low and loud. I am always struck by how loud the noise is from the sky in Northern Virginia. The only thing that drowns it out is the noise from the Beltway and the ancillary highways.

Dulles is, to put it mildly, not a very special place. It may be a useful and even arguably important place. But special? No way.

And now, after conducting the research for this chapter and writing it all out, I cannot possibly look at this airport the same way again. For me, Dulles will always be synonymous with the oppression of Black Americans and state-based tyranny. One wonders how many other American places have been destroyed because of institutionalized white supremacy. I bet it's a lot. And their racist histories have, by and large, been eradicated or willingly forgotten.

VII.

And so that's the story of Willard, Virginia. Its story is as tragic as that of the Minisink and the other places included in this book. But it was once a real place, full of all the beauties of everyday American life. It was once a place for displaced Black people to seek solace and protection. It was, perhaps, a potential paradise.

I'd thus like to offer the words of Toni Morrison once again, this time from the end of her novel Paradise. This book chronicles the violent upheavals following Black migration out of the South and into the dusty towns of Oklahoma. This is the place where Laura Nelson was lynched from a railroad bridge, still dressed in her calico dress, swaying next to the dead body of her son.

It is important to note that many Black residents of the South chose to move to places like Oklahoma precisely to avoid the kind of fate that awaited Ms. Nelson. But as this chapter has endeavored to show you, the history of Black America is a long story of constant displacement and disappointment. Oklahoma – like the town of Willard – was thought to be a paradise, a place where Black people could live unmolested and free.

But, as it always seems to go, these potential paradises turn out to be living hells. As Morrison writes,

She had another question: When will they return? When will they reappear, with blazing eyes, war paint and huge hands to rip up and stomp down this prison calling itself a town. A town that tried to ruin her grandfather, succeeded in swallowing her mother and almost broken her own self. A backward noplace ruled by men whose power to control was out of control and who had the nerve to say who could live and who not and where; who had seen in lively, free, unarmed females the mutiny of the mares and so got rid of them. She hoped with all her heart that the women were out there, darkly burnished, biding their time, brass-metaling their nails, filing their incisors – but out there. Which is to say she hoped for a miracle.

I, too, hope for a miracle. I hope for a time when this country will fully – and finally – live up to its values. I hope that white Americans will take the time to truly come to terms with the racist legacy of the United States and work to bring about the kind of change that will stop atrocities like the loss of Willard from ever happening again. It's only then that we will ever find paradise.

Where It All Begins:
Waterloo, New Jersey

His mind all day flew ahead of the train to the little town...
where he had spent his boyhood and youth. As the train passed
the...River, with its curiously carved cliffs, its cold, dark, swift-swirl-
ing water eating slowly under the cedar-clothed banks, Howard began to feel curious little movements of the heart, like a lover as he
nears his sweetheart.
— Hamlin Garland, "Up the Coulee"

The nest, I say, to you, I Maximus, say
Under the hand, as I see it, over the waters
From this place where I am, where I hear,
Can still hear

From where I carry you a feather
As though, sharp, I picked up,
In the afternoon delivered you
A jewel,
     It flashing more than a wing,
Than any old romantic thing,
Than memory, than place,
Than anything other than that which you carry
— Charles Olson, "I, Maximus of Gloucester, to You"

I.

In 1959, a teenage couple rode their bicycles to a big steel bridge that spanned the Musconetcong River. They hid their bikes in the woods and snuck onto the bridge. They took care not to be seen; after all, this was private property owned by Waterloo Village, a historic town converted into an entertainment and wedding venue. The operators of the site were notorious for chasing off the locals who liked to party and play on the grounds. Knowing this, the couple had arrived right around dusk to avoid being spotted.

Once on the bridge, the sixteen-year-old boy jumped into the dark turbid waters of the river and yelled up at the girl to do the same. Frightened by the height, she hesitated while her boyfriend treaded water waiting for her. Finally – after what seemed to be ages – she jumped...and landed right on his head, almost drowning him in the process.

In the early 1980s, two young men in their early twenties parked a car at the end of a dirt road just an hour or two before midnight. They assembled their fishing rods and took care not to be seen. They climbed over the guardrail of Interstate 80 and ran across the eastbound and westbound lanes. Once on the other side of the highway, they crept to the far bank of the Musconetcong. The threw out topwater lures in the hopes of enticing largemouth bass while a wedding reception was taking place on the other side of the river. They caught several fish and managed not to be seen... until one of them noticed that a large watersnake had latched on to one of the fish on their stringer. Frightened, the young man threw the entire stringer of fish – seven or eight big bass in total – into the river and yelled. Someone from Waterloo Village heard the commotion and began to yell back at them. The young men then turned and ran and climbed back onto Route 80 and bolted across to the safety of the other side. Once back at the car, one of them realized he had left his fishing pole behind. He waited a good half an hour and then repeated the journey, successfully retrieving his rod while not being caught.

In the late 1980s, a married couple left their young son with the wife's mother and father and headed to Waterloo Village to attend a concert. They were there to see the Allman Brothers Band, the famous jam band that the husband absolutely loved. For once, they were there for a sanctioned event, so they did not have to take care not to be seen. In the field a stone's throw from the ancient village itself, the couple listened to the long and rambling guitar solos and dynamic piano interludes and Gregg Allman's voice of pain and suffering for three hours. It rained the whole time, but they didn't care. By the time "Whipping Post" played, they were soaked and jubilant and ready to head home.

II.

The individuals in the above vignettes are as follows: the couple on the bridge are my maternal grandparents, the young rule-breaking fishermen are my father and my uncle, and the concert-going married couple are my mother and father. The young son, of course, is me.

My family has lived in or near northwestern New Jersey for several centuries. Indeed, they were some of the first white settlers of that region. And, in classic American fashion, many of them have continued to live and work in that exact spot. They stayed so long, in fact, that they spent all this time in and around Waterloo Village without even realizing that many of their forbearers were actually buried in the cemetery of the town's United Methodist Church. Nathaniel Best, Sarah Ike, Jacob Ike and Sarah Tyger, and others all gave life to this family, but by the twentieth century, they weren't even a distant memory anymore.

How does this happen? How do people lose track of their ancestors in this way? How does one family spend so much time in a single spot, so much so that their own history is tightly wound with the history of that place? Why do they keep returning to Waterloo – to this day – like iron flecks to a magnet? The answers to these questions provide a detailed and introspective gaze into the making and losing of a quintessential American place: the iconic northwestern New Jersey historic site of Waterloo Village.

III.

The first of my ancestors to arrive in northwest New Jersey in the area that would later become Waterloo were farmers. They settled at the base of the Appalachian Mountains in the gentle rolling foothills of what is now Sussex County. At the time, the area was completely forested. It was truly the frontier, with towering chestnut trees dominating the skyline and gray wolves and mountain lions roaming the forested understory.

It would have been an intimidating place to move. With no nearby towns or cities, these individuals were truly on their own. Furthermore, the area wasn't initially conducive to farming. It had to be made that way.

In part because of the last glaciation, the northwest New Jersey area is littered with moraine, a substance otherwise known as glacial debris. To understand how moraine develops, try imagining a wall of ice over a mile high moving ever so slowly over the ground. Its massive weight allows it to scourge the landscape and pick up rock after rock after rock. Then, when the glacier ultimately melts, it leaves behind this rocky legacy.

So, to create conditions for optimal farming, the early white settlers of northwest New Jersey had to not only saw down gigantic trees, cut them up, and pull out their stumps, they also had to remove thousands upon thousands of rocks from the ground. And they did it. Somehow. Without modern mechanized machinery. Somehow, they did it.

And they lined their properties with the rocks, separating cornfields from wheatfields and barleyfields from hopsfields. These rock walls still stand to this day. Drive through the region and you will be sure to see the results of this massive undertaking still slithering through the rocky woods like stone effigies to some otherworldly snake god.

The early farmers were mostly in it for subsistence. The trees they felled provided the timber to build their homes. Corn fed their cattle and wheat fed their families. Barley and hops helped make early forms of American beer. They slaughtered hogs for the winter and preserved their crops by building ice houses and root cellars in the ground. Anything they had left over they would sell or trade to bring in new goods.

It wasn't a glorious lifestyle, but it worked. Each member of the family had deep value; they were all needed to work – girl and boy, man and woman. The bonds formed between them would have been extremely strong. And when they went to church on Sundays they would gather with families from nearby. Children that played together outside of the chapels would grow up to become marriage partners, repeating the processes of their parents and eventually giving birth to a new country.

Indeed, it wasn't a glorious lifestyle, but I believe in my heart these were fundamentally happy people. I can still hear their laughter when I walk through their old fields.

IV.

On a cold winter day about a year ago, I brought my wife and kids to Waterloo. My children had never been there; I took the occasion to explain the concept of "ancestor" to them. "You know how your grandma had a mommy and a daddy? Well, they also had mommies and daddies, and on and on and on. People fall in love, it's what we do, and it creates a line that goes back forever." My five-year-old nodded in agreement. My two-year-old threw another rock in the canal. Such is parenthood.

My daughter expressed an interest in visiting her ancestors. "I want to meet them, daddy," she said. I explained that they were dead, but that we were about to do the next best thing. "Well, I can show you where and how they lived in this place. Then, we can visit their graves in the churchyard. While we walk around, try to imagine them living and working here."

We started by walking along the Morris Canal, the watery artery that gave life to Waterloo. "Boats moved coal from Pennsylvania to New York City along this canal. It's not a river; it's a manmade channel that helped our ancestors trade with places really far away from where they lived." We made our way to a beautifully preserved lock. "Here is where they moved the boats up and down, so that they could go either direction. That's really what makes a canal special. You can only go one direction on a river; not so on a canal." I pointed to a cleared tract of land on the far side of the lock: "That hill over there was known as an inclined plane, and also helped them move stuff."

We moved on. Soon, we came to the gristmill. "Notice this chute that's diverting water from the big pool above the lock," I said. "They used this to power the mill. You have to remember, they didn't have electricity like we did. There are no lightswitches or electrical outlets in these buildings. They needed to harvest the energy from the running water, which in turn helped them grind wheatgrain and make things like flour. You know, not flowers like the bees like but the white stuff we use to make cookies." Both children nodded vigorously in agreement about the cookies.

We continued our walk through town. Many of the buildings have been restored, but many still have not. Waterloo has something of a schizophrenic personality. On one hand, it's been touched by the hand of restoration and wears the appearance of a living history museum; on the other, it looks like a straight up ghost town. As with most lost places, it actively seeks to defy categorization.

My wife explained some of the basics about its architecture to the children. We debated the differences between Late Victorian and Second Empire. The children chased after some robins that had landed in the yard of one of the dilapidated houses.

Eventually we circled back and headed for our final destination: the Methodist Church. "Do people still go to church here?" my daughter asked me. "They do," I replied. "It's absolutely amazing, but this congregation has been here continuously since our ancestors lived and worshiped here."

We walked to the cemetery and began looking for our people. We found Nathaniel and Sarah Best first. "These are your great-great-great-great-great grandparents. They had a daughter who had the same name as you," I said. My oldest daughter rushed up to the grave and came back holding a gorgeous birdfeather. "I think they left this for me, Dad!" she said excitedly. "Maybe they knew you were coming and really loved feathers," my wife replied. My daughter hugged it to her chest. She still has it: it's anchored in a small jar on a shelf over her bed. Who are we to say ghosts aren't real? Try telling that to my daughter. She's got a feather to show you as proof of ghostly reality.

We next found Sarah's parents' gravestone. "And these are your great-great-great-great-great-great grandparents. They lived a really long time for people who were born in the 1700s. They must have been really strong and healthy people. This grandma of yours had eight children, who all grew up to adulthood. That's amazing!" To this my daughter asked why she only has one sister. My wife and I changed the subject.

Before we left and headed back to the car I suggested that we thank our ancestors for everything they gave us. "We wouldn't be here if it wasn't for them," I said. We said our thank yous, walked back to the canal, and followed it to our car.

V.

The partially restored Waterloo that my family and I visited takes for its historical baseline the town's time as a waypoint on the Morris Canal. It is easy to overlook the importance of canals to the development of the United States. Most of them have been filled in and almost none are currently active. If you say the word canal to an average American, they will automatically think of the world's most geopolitically important one down in Panama.

But yet, there's a compelling case to be made that the United States as we know it would not exist if not for the nineteenth-century canal system. The most famous of this era is the Erie Canal, a 363-mile behemoth immortalized by the folk song "Low Bridge." The song, like many other folk tunes, encapsulates the experience of canal-life better than most histories. Consider the following verses:

We've hauled some barges in our day

Filled with lumber, coal, and hay
And every inch of the way we know
From Albany to Buffalo

Low bridge, everybody down
Low bridge cause we're coming to a town
And you'll always know your neighbor
You'll always know your pal
If you've ever navigated on the Erie Canal

Get up there Sal, we've passed a lock,
Fifteen years on the Erie Canal
And we'll make Rome before six o'clock
Fifteen years on the Erie Canal

One more trip and back we'll go
Through the rain and sleet and snow
And every inch of the way I we know
From Albany to Buffalo

It was the second commodity listed in the above first verse that powered the Morris Canal that ran through Waterloo Village. Bargemen moved anthracite coal from central Pennsylvania to the New York City (NYC) metropolitan area all day, every day. In fact, there is no doubt that coal from Centralia – the subject of chapter two – made its way along this very route. And the City desperately needed it; its growth during the nineteenth century was enormous. Although this next fact may seem unbelievable, I guarantee you that it is true: New York City went from a population of tens of thousands at the dawn of the nineteenth century to literally millions by the end of it. And these people – immigrant, middle, and upper classes, all – needed coal to heat their homes.

Beyond providing the substance that heated mansions and tenement buildings alike, New York relied on anthracite to fuel the blast furnaces that made the steel that was rapidly transforming the city. If you look at the NYC skyline today, many of those buildings are still supported by steel that was literally made possible by the Morris Canal and the workers who toiled along its path.

As the folk song above demonstrates, the towns located along the canal were of the utmost importance. The provided places for tired bargemen to sleep, workers who operated the locks, repair-shops for broken equipment, and general stores that provided anything and everything someone might need to successfully complete the journey.

And it turns out that my ancestors' hometown was located almost precisely halfway along the Morris Canal. Such serendipitous positioning is what helped transform the sleepy hamlet of Andover Forge into the bustling town that we now call Waterloo (its name was changed to celebrate Napoleon's defeat early in the nineteenth century).

Nathaniel and Sarah Best lived in Waterloo during the canal's heyday. As such, it would have formed the background of their daily lives. On this barge, anthracite coal, on this one iron ore, on another ice, and on yet another whiskey. I wonder if they ever journeyed on the canal themselves. Although the Morris Canal was almost predominantly a commercial affair, I have read reports that indicated some people took trips on it just to see the surrounding areas. Maybe Nathaniel took a young Sarah for a ride on an icebarge to see the big city being built only fifty miles to the east. What an early date that would have been!

Maybe, after they started their family, they took their children for short rides to Hackettstown (the site of my own birth) or to Dover (the biggest town in the area and the site of my parents' births). They could have used the canal to seek medical care in more established areas, or to visit family who had left the country-side for the rapidly growing urban areas located nearby. I'm willing to bet that they did these things. The canal was a lifegiver in more ways than one.

The comings and goings of the canal brought economic life to this little slice of northwest New Jersey for over a century. But by the second decade of the twentieth century the railroad had rendered the canal useless and people began moving out of Waterloo Village. Most of my ancestors scattered to places like Randolph or Andover. Some stayed relatively close by in Stanhope and Netcong. But almost no one was living in Waterloo by the time the Great Depression hit. It was a ghost town, full of dilapidated buildings and an unused canal.

Soon after, though, it was destined to enter into one of its many afterlives.

VI.

In an ironic twist of fate, the Great Depression might have contributed to the survival of Waterloo. Because of its centralized location on the Lackawanna Railroad, Waterloo became a squatters' town during the 1930s and 1940s. It's hard to put a number on their total population, but quite a few hobos called the village home during these decades.

There is a myth out there that the hobos repaired the abandoned Waterloo buildings and prevented them from falling into ruin; the state, according to this myth, chose not to demolish Waterloo because these people were actively living in it. Therefore, the hobos saved Waterloo Village. It is my belief, however, that this myth is misguided at best. The truth is that Waterloo wasn't torn down because the cost of doing so was prohibitive. In general, demolition is cheaper than construction, but it is still expensive. In this period, no entity had any extra funds laying around that could be devoted to such an endeavor. Because of the horrible unemployment situation, Depression-era state budgets were an absolute mess. No one had the time or the energy to do anything about a random abandoned town in the hinterlands of New Jersey. The hobos were just lucky that there was a place for them to live that literally wasn't outside. For me, the myth is reversed. By providing them with stable shelter, Waterloo allowed the hobos to survive the Great Depression.

Think of it this way. Riding the rails was a quintessential Depression-era activity. And although images of hobos jumping off boxcars in the American West are engrained in our cultural memory, the practice occurred everywhere in the United States – including in New Jersey. In the mid-Atlantic and elsewhere, unemployment percentages neared 50% of the working population during the Depression. Out of work men – particularly young unmarried men – chose to ride back and forth from Phillipsburg to Newark along the Lackawanna Railroad. Along the way they looked for work where they could find it. They scrounged along the railroad looking for coal that fell off the cars. The scavenged iron ore. They stole food and whiskey. They did whatever they needed to do to survive. And survive they did. In the aftermath of the Second World War, the hobos who received shelter at Waterloo were able to re-enter American society. Many of them might have died if not for the abandoned town they briefly called home.

It is during this period that, I believe, my family lost their connection to Waterloo. An economic depression of immense size is the kind of event that disrupts everything, including a family's ties to a specific place. Who has the time to worry about the past when the present forces a daily battle for survival? Although my family continued to live near their ancestral hometown, memory of their deep connection to it faded. When my grandfather was born in 1945, no one in my family knew that the hobo-infested abandoned village nearby housed the bones of their forefathers.

As my family lost touch with their heritage, another wave of human life and experience had washed over the old canal town. As the US entered the postwar golden age, the scene was set for an altogether different reinvention of this lost place.

VII.

In the late 1960s, a few local businessmen founded the Waterloo Foundation for the Arts – a nonprofit entity that was designed to raise funds for the restoration of the village. One of the Foundation's first acts was to make Waterloo a living history site. Local folks and members of the Foundation acted as blacksmiths and canalmen and millworkers, entertaining school children for several decades. Both my mother and my father experienced the living history era of Waterloo when they were children. Of course, neither of them knew about any of their family members' connections to the place. My mother probably walked right next to her great-great-great grandparents' grave without even knowing it.

The Foundation quickly learned that restoration is quite pricey and that they needed alternative revenue streams. Grants and donations weren't going to cut it. They came up with a really unique and effective idea: turn some of the land outside of the village into a concert venue. So, in the old fields that my ancestors used to grow wheat and hops, Waterloo erected a stage and leveled ground for a parking lot. The first concert happened in the late 1970s.

The acts that played the Waterloo stage comprise a drool-worthy list for any fan of American popular music. Here's a sample: Muddy Waters, Johnny Cash, The Beach Boys, Arlo Guthrie, Roy

Orbison, Bob Dylan, Neil Young, the Steve Miller Band, Stevie Ray Vaughan, John Denver, Ray Charles, and Ringo Starr. Like… oh my God. There really aren't bigger names than this. In addition, acts from the alternative rock revolution of the early 1990s also played at Waterloo, including Nine Inch Nails, Jane's Addiction, Rage Against The Machine, Pearl Jam, Soundgarden, Red Hot Chili Peppers, Blink-182, and Alice in Chains. It's a veritable who's who of alternative rock. I'd like to think these bands – at the very least – shook the gravestones of the Bests.

Waterloo also played host to country acts, the musical genre favored by my grandparents. So, several decades after falling love on the steel bridge over the Musconetcong River, my grandparents went to see Charley Pride play at Waterloo. Again, while they swayed to the beautiful lyrics of "Kiss An Angel Good Morning," they had no idea that they were dancing on land that once belonged to their family.

And yet, I still feel like the land does belong to them, as it does to me and to my daughters. I don't mean to imply that we have some kind of ancient legal claim over Waterloo and its environs. Or that we have squatters' rights to it. That being said, I do believe that a deep-seated spiritual attachment to place can transcend the boundaries of time and space. That it can be passed down, even without conscious knowledge of its existence. Is it any coincidence that my cousin regularly took her son to walk the grounds at Waterloo, even before I told her that her ancestors lived and were buried there? Is it a coincidence that my wife and I considered it as a venue for our wedding? Was that birdfeather left on Nathaniel and Sarah Best's grave really the result of chance? I don't think so. Waterloo runs deep in our blood. It's our home. It's where it all began.

VIII.

Not everyone is as lucky as we are. Most people don't have their ancestral hometown preserved in any fashion whatsoever, especially if said town is in a rural area. And even if that hometown is actually a city, what ends up happening is, well, demolition. The New York of 2021 bears little to no resemblance to the New York of 1921 or 1821 or 1721. That's what cities do: space is at a premium, so buildings get torn down and new ones erected. As a consequence, the past is erased.

But Waterloo remains. Currently, it is part of the Allamuchy State Park. As such, it is supported by state money and various grants and will be for the foreseeable future. The word in Northwest New Jersey is that they plan to bring back music festivals, if not the rollicking Lollapaloozas of the early '90s (which, to be honest, is probably a good thing).

And, to me, this is important. Waterloo is so much more than a canaltown or a ghost town or a squatters' paradise. It is a place of love. It is a place where early Americans met, fell in love, got married, and raised families. It's where their descendants broke the rules and fell in love while swinging in the air above the River. It's where generations of lovers flocked to the Waterloo stage to hear their favorite musicians play.

When viewed this way, Waterloo Village transform into a museum of that most important and foundational human emotion: romantic love.

Benediction

"If the way which I have pointed out as leading to this result seems exceedingly hard, it may nevertheless be discovered. Needs must it be hard, since it is so seldom found. How would it be possible, if salvation were ready to our hand, and could without great labour be found, that it should be by almost all men neglected? But all things excellent are as difficult as they are rare."

— Benedict de Spinoza, Ethics

We've come to the end. It is no longer my path, but yours. I implore you to go out into the world and search for lost places. Do not be afraid of the dust and destruction. Enter into the abyss, no matter the terror. Confront the ghosts that you find there. Listen to them speak. Open your soul to their voices.

Bring the lost places that you find home with you. Meditate on them. Give them light. And above all else, tell their stories. If you do all of this, you too will become a keeper of lost places.

Acknowledgements

I would like to thank each and every family member, friend, colleague, and student who has listened to me talk about this project for the last several years. It has been a long road and I never would have been able to travel it without all of your love and support.

In particular, I would like to thank my wife Jackie and my children Emmaline and Phebe. Thank you for letting me drag you to research trips to ghost towns and into abandoned buildings in the middle of nowhere. I promise that the next book will include some nicer locations with less depressing histories.

I would like to thank my mother Debbie, her husband Keith, my father Marvin, and his wife Tracey. You all are the foundation for my success.

Thank you to my sister Kristin, her husband Lee, my niece Madison, my nephew Landon, and my sister Jenna. Without all of you, the chapter on Haydenville would never have been completed.

Thank you to my grandmother Isabel and my Uncle Howie for letting me tell your stories about Waterloo Village.

A gigantic thank you is owed to Greg Miller. Our (slightly tipsy) discussions deep into the night about the Minisink are what set this whole project in motion.

Thank you to Jack, Mary, and Mike Miller. Mike, your presence is everywhere in this book.

Thank you as well to my friends Lauren and Will, my fellow teenage Pocono tourist industry workers, for your reminiscences of our time working at Mountain Manor.

Thank you to my bestie Helene – I don't know what I'd do without you. I hope the next time I see you I'll be able to hand you a copy of this book.

I offer a special thank you to my friends Chelsea Rathburn and Jim May. The two of you showed me that I have value as a writer and helped me discover the poetry inside of me. Your encouragement in the early days of this project helped steer me in the right direction and helped set the tone for the entire book.

I would like to also thank all of my Young Harris College colleagues. In particular, I want to thank Eloise Whisenhunt, Mark Rollins, and Jason Pierce, my superiors at Young Harris College. This may not be the kind of book you expected out of me when you hired me as an early American literature scholar, but your support for this project provided me with the professional backing necessary to writerly success.

Thank you, as well, to Rob Cohen and Christine Roth, the publishers of this book and now my friends. Thank you for taking a chance on me. I hope I've made you proud.

No writer emerges out of this world without having incredible teachers. To my undergraduate mentors, Michael Drexler and Saundra Morris: thank you for everything, you took my diamond-in-the-rough nature and helped make me into the person I am today. To my graduate mentors, Tom Augst, Liz McHenry, Jennifer Baker, and Bryan Waterman...this may not be the dissertation you spent so many hours reading and editing, but it is a book that is reflective of the type of scholar you made out of me. The influences of the four of you are everywhere in this book.

And finally, I'd like to offer a profound and deep thank you to my friend and one-time co-author, Rebecca Cheong. You believed in my writing before anyone else did. You gave me the confidence to step out of academic writing and try my hand at something different. This book would not exist if not for you. So thank you, Rebecca.

Printed in the USA
CPSIA information can be obtained
at www.ICGtesting.com
LVHW041148160524
780333LV00011B/320